HOW TO WRITE YOUR BOOK –
BOOK 3 Crossing The Finish Line

From an Idea...

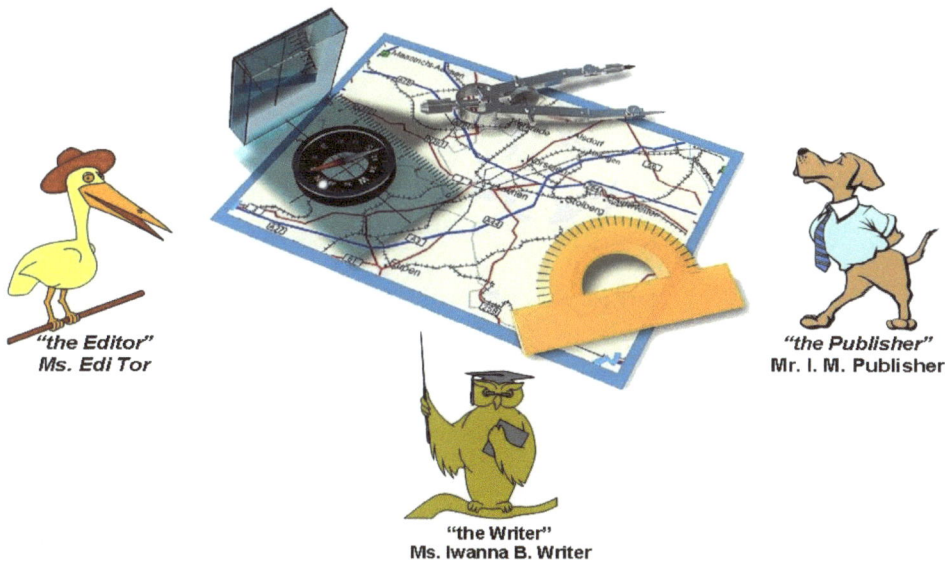

"the Editor"
Ms. Edi Tor

"the Publisher"
Mr. I. M. Publisher

"the Writer"
Ms. Iwanna B. Writer

to your Finished Story

as narrated by
The Three Wise Guides

Bobbi Madry & Francine Barish-Stern

Published By Golden Quill Press

a division of Barish-Stern Ltd.

P.O. Box 83

Troutville, VA 24175

Copyright ©2015

Bobbi Madry & Francine Barish-Stern

ISBN 978-0-9847330-3-3

Cover by Art on Gold, Troutville VA.

Interior Design by Kenneth A Bray, Troutville VA.

Printed by CreateSpace, An Amazon.com Company
Available from Amazon.com and other retail outlets
Available from Amazon.com and other online stores
Available from Amazon.com and other book stores
Available from Amazon.com, CreateSpace.com, and other retail outlets
A reference to an Amazon review
Available on Kindle and other devices
Available on Kindle and other retail outlets
Available on Kindle and other book stores
Available on Kindle and online stores

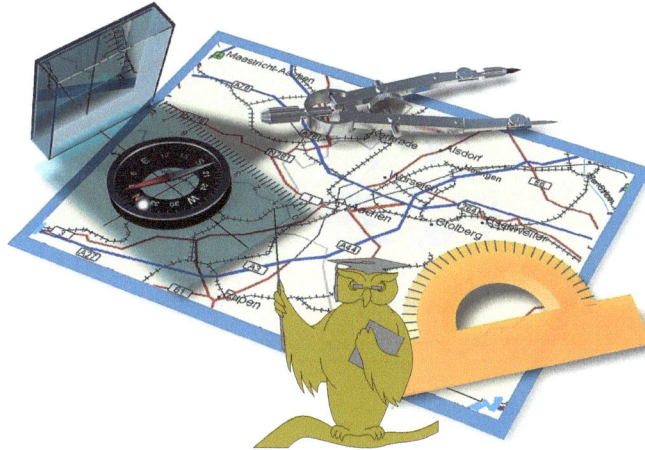

TABLE OF CONTENTS

GUIDE TO ROAD SIGNS

Writing Map 1   **Trip Signs:** These Writing Map Signs will identify each new chapter of your journey as a color coordinated Writing Map. Think of these signs as the Welcome Sign you see when entering a new state that you must pass through to get to your final destination. Each sign will also correspond to the downloadable Extra Bonus Travel Forms.

DO IT NOW! **Map Sign:** This sign will alert you to ATTRACTIONS worth stopping at. Visiting will help to reinforce chapter information.

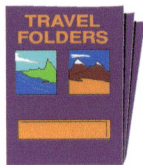

Travel Folders: Throughout this book you'll be prompted to create folders. We suggest setting up physical File Folders as well as computer files.

The Forms are divided into Example and Exercise. A Feature of The Examples is that they follow an actual book, Golden Quill Press' "Code 47 to BREV Force."

Suitcase: Finally we have to pack for the voyage— So use this SUITCASE to Pack all materials, supplies, file folders, extra forms and any other materials you will need to travel *"From an Idea...to your Finished Story."* Each chapter review will tell you what to put in your suitcase. Remember Your Suitcase is also an organizer file. It should contain everything you'll need and can be a physical file and a computer file.

Pit Stops: This book also offers interactive Service Stations placed strategically along your route to assist you in making those necessary pit stops. You will find: Web Support — E-mail Tech Support — Forums — and Benefits all designed to help you get back on the road. Look for these Road Signs when you need that pit stop—

We also suggest that whenever you want to remember some point we've made or in order to trigger something specific you want to remember when you begin writing, you create a **Map Pin**. Your map pin is basically the Map Number, Page Number and Topic. Using **Map Pins will help you easily** locate that information, and get you moving on your voyage.

Travel Kit Form   **Travel Forms:** At the end of each Chapter you will find additional forms called Travel Kit Forms- You may also be prompted to use them along your journey by

We strongly recommend you use them at every opportunity to further your writing experience.

Writing is hard work— you began that work in Book 1 so now let's get on the Super Highway and Write, Write, Write!.

BON VOYAGE !!!

Take Your Sentences to the Writing Mechanic!

When you need to fix your Sentence Puncture—ation

Mechanic-- ism is that Good Writing?

"the Editor"
Ms. Edi Tor

"the Writer"
Ms. Iwanna B. Writer

"the Publisher"
Mr. I. M. Publisher

Writing Map 8

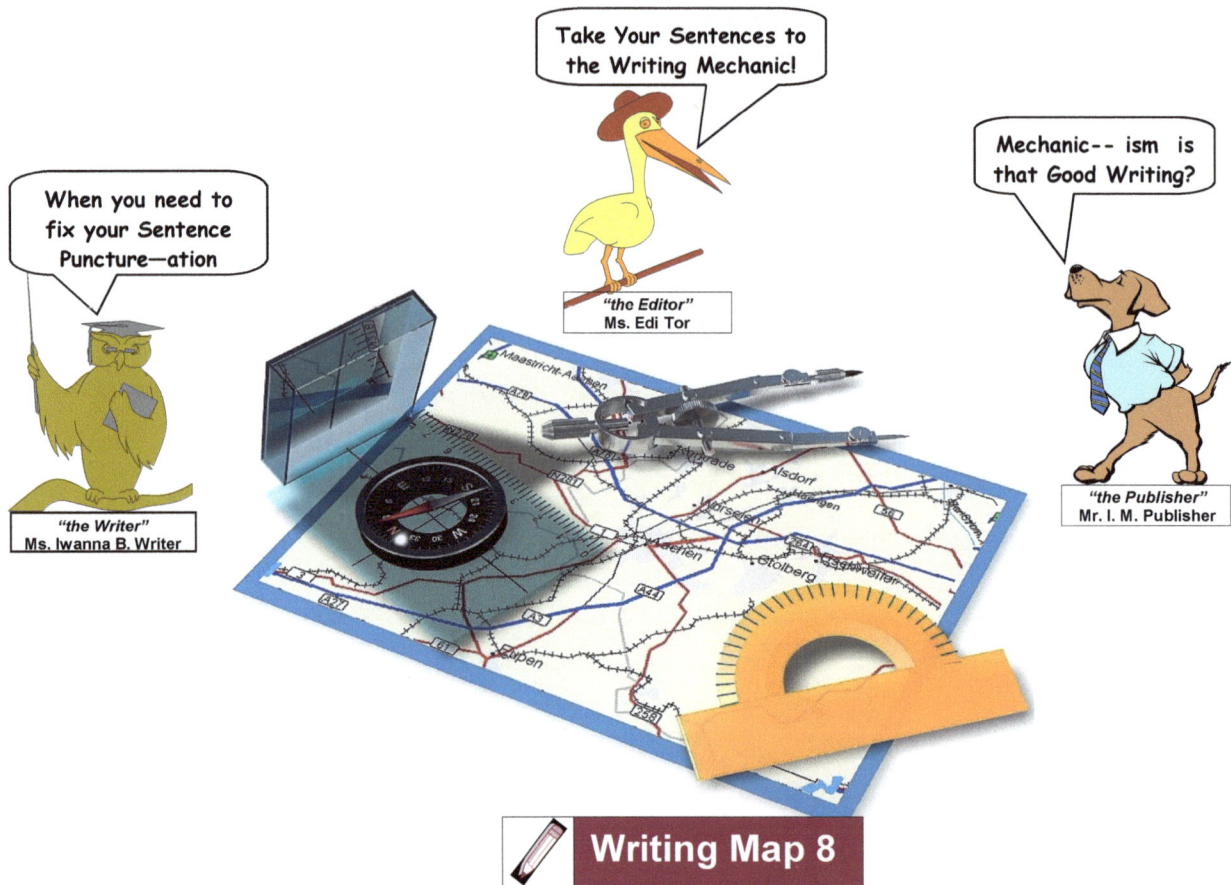

MECHANIC--ISM'S OF WRITING

Our editor guide Ms. Edi Tor will be taking you through the mechanics of writing. Even though we call your first formal story writing a "draft," you still need to understand the mechanics. A first draft is your rough plan, put down on paper with the intention of being revised into the final manuscript.

Our Writing Guides Have Issued this Draft Alert!

You may want your First Draft to be your finished book, but you need to be prepared for editing, revising and rewriting!

1

Writing Map 8

Some writers can write a book the first time, but most writers need several drafts; editing and revisions. So let's assume that the first writing is a draft! When you are traveling on your writing journey and feel a "draft," you would stop and let a trained mechanic examine the problem. So here's what the Mechanics of Writing recommend to diagnose your Draft.

Choose Your Writing Venue

Writing Long Hand:	Writing on a Typewriter	Writing on a Computer (Example uses MS WORD)
• Lined paper 8.5 X 11 • Write on every other line • Write on only one side of the page • Indent 5 Spaces: beginning lines, quotes and new paragraphs • Number your pages • Start a separate page for each new chapter • Make copies whenever possible (copies can be made at libraries or post offices or office supply retail places that have copy machines) • **Drafts** Make up a Draft Folder and always put your work in there (Note: Final Manuscripts must be in typewritten or computerized format)	• Blank, White 8.5 X 11 paper • Margins – 1 inch around • Indent 5 spaces: beginning lines, quotes & new paragraphs • Double Space • Type on only one side of the page • Number pages • Start a separate page for each new chapter 1/3 of the way down • Make copies (Use carbon or NCR paper, or go to the library or post office, or office supply retail places that have copy machines) • **Drafts** Make a Draft Folder and always put your work in there	• Open Word & start with a blank document • Go to "File" (top far left) left click to open – then click on Page Set-up – (this opens a window) under Margins you will see top, bottom, left and right. You can set your margins at 1" around and be sure your page orientation is set to Portrait • As soon as you have finished your page preferences, save your work. Saving the first time –establish a folder "Draft" either in My Documents or on your Desktop. Be sure to Save your work there as you go. • Start a separate page for each new chapter and begin 1/3 of the way down the page with your Chapter # or Chapter Title • Under Format (in the top header) left click, then click on font – Choose: Arial or Times Roman, Font Style: Regular, font Size: 12 and color Automatic or Black. Under Format (in the top header) left click, then click on Paragraph—Under Line Spacing click on Double • Indent 5 Spaces: beginning lines, quotes, and new paragraphs • When you finish your writing sessions save your work and follow whatever procedures you use to back-up your work • Blank white 8.5 X 11 paper (for draft printing) • Print on only one side of the page • Print only on White Paper – Black Ink

2

Now that Our Mechanic has given you the spec's for set up— to begin writing your first Draft, you can begin to use the Mechanics Technical Manual found below which includes directions for using different techniques for beginning your story.

Techniques from the Mechanic

Writers use many different devices when beginning a story. If you want your reader to go further than the first ten pages this is your "15 Minutes of Fame." The beginning of your story can make or break you. So let's make it so exciting the reader can't put it down. There are many openers that work, but of course you need to find the one that works for your story. Here are our Mechanics Choices:

CHARACTER
Open with the main character doing something that gets to the meat of the story: saving the world, going into pre-mature labor, committing murder, or falling off a cliff
> **Example:** Brad knew he was wrong, but all he could think of was, *if I can fix this, I can destroy Controller and save Jonathan's life.*

If your character is going to save the world you could begin with the action
> **Example:** *Brad had to make the most of his jail time. If he could just get into Controller's network, he knew he could get his revenge.*

Or try fast paced dialog specific to the action
> **Example:** "Evie what's going on?"
> "Oh, Rick. I believed this was a real job, but now they have pictures of me that they are threatening to use on the internet..."
> "I won't let them hurt you. Sheila knows a lot of people and..."
> "Sheila!" she screamed. "I should've known better that to trust you! Just go away and leave me alone." she ran out the door.
> *What the...! Evie, Sheila they're all crazy. Or maybe it's me?*

Bring your character into the scene
> **Example:** Island Falls was beautiful at this time of year, but Dr. Schmidt wasn't interested in the beautiful scenery Vivian and Martin pointed out. All he wanted was to get into the lab, get what he came for and leave.

SCENES

Setting a scene can be enticing to a reader. Be sure you establish the reason for the scene.
> **Example:** Vid-Mart was the latest electronics super store to open at Compustock Mall. Brad enjoyed working there because all the great looking girls from both colleges in the town eventually came in for something.

DESCRIPTION

Describing the day, a character, or event is another way to begin. Don't get too long winded on description if it doesn't move the story along.

> **Example:** The leaves were kicking up in the wind, on that chilly autumn day. Martin knew he'd soon be raking up the dirt that his lies would leave.

TIME PERIODS

You can begin your story in the past, present or future. You can also start with a chapter about something that happened long ago or will happen in the future, that seemingly has nothing to do with your story. You can lay the groundwork for the event that will be pivotal in your story., but you wouldn't even make mention to that event until you were ready to tie things together later. That later chapter is called the Pivotal moment.

> **Example:** Opening Chapter --1912 The Titanic sails from England and sinks
>
> Next Chapter — 2008 Martin and Vivian two interns meet at the Science Institute

Pivotal event - Later Chapter — Martin and Vivian marry and are planning their honeymoon. He suggests a cruise. She nearly faints at the thought. Through her tears she tells him her grandfather was killed on the Titanic. He can't believe it, his Grandmother was too!

DIALOGUE

A phrase that will be repeated or will have significance throughout the story

> **Example:** "<R U the 1?>"

Or, introducing a conversation, mid-stream

> **Example:** "I understand that emotions limit our abilities, but I can't help it."

No matter how you begin your story it's essential that you hook the reader and that you set the tone and style of the story, right from the beginning. Examine the writings of modern uthors such as: Jeffrey Archer, Patricia Cornwell, Tom Clancy, Clive Cussler, John Grisham, Tami Hoag, Johanna Lindsey, James Patterson, Sidney Sheldon, Danielle Steele or return to the classics of: Jane Austin, Charlotte Bronte, Charles Dickens, Mark Twain or Leo Tolstoy, but whoever you choose, look for the hook and the tone and style they set.

CHAPTERS

Years ago if you would have asked how long a chapter should be, the answer may have been - - the longer the better. Today that's no longer the case. Recently we have even seen a long time best seller: The Da Vinci Code by Dan Brown, where a chapter is a page long, or less. Using good judgment is probably the best answer. If you're moving your story from: one central character to another, to a new location or a different time period, these changes should be reflected by a new chapter. You can also use chapters to create cliff hanger endings or to take your story in another direction.

MECHANICS MANUAL OF PUCTUATIONI

When you speak face to face with another person you have more than words alone to make your meaning clear to the listener. Your facial expressions, gestures, body movements, tone of voice, and pauses all influence the meanings of words you speak. But when you write you don't have all of that going for you, so what do you do?

The primary aim of writing is to communicate with the reader, and this is why punctuation — a kind of roadmap — was established. The rules of punctuation have been standardized by educators, writers, and editors for more than a hundred years, to make writing as clear and coherent as the spoken word. When you use the right punctuation, the reader can understand words and their meanings. For example, when speaking, you pause and hesitate, and when writing, you use the comma to pause, and the period as a full stop.

Too much punctuation can be as confusing as too little. You should use just enough to make your story flow easily and as naturally as if you were speaking. Reading your sentences aloud will help you see where you may need to correct punctuation.

The Mechanics Manual of Punctuation
Note: For easy reference; punctuation will be put in
BOLD RED

Period (.) is used at the end of a complete sentence. It is also used as the end mark for initials and many abbreviations.

> Mrs. Smith sent her manuscript to a publisher in Trenton, N.J.
> The editor was impressed by J. T.'s short story.

Comma (,) is used inside sentences, in places where one would pause while speaking. It is also used to set off many phrases and clauses, and should be used before end quotation marks.

> Tom found his car in the parking lot, only to realize he had lost his keys.
> "I have a new bike," John said.

Question Mark (?) is used at the end of an inquiry, or a sentence that asks something.

> "Do you know who won the baseball game?"
> "How did the editor like your manuscript?"

Exclamation Point (!) Is used to convey stronger-than-usual emotion or urgency. It can also follow certain interjections instead of a comma.

> "How dare you say that!"
> " Hey! That's my car!"

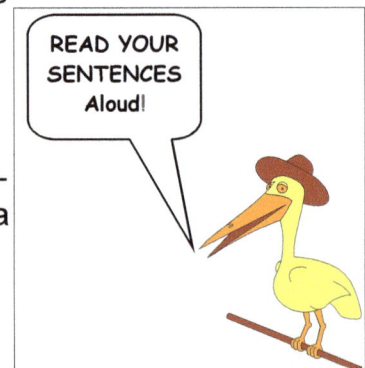

READ YOUR SENTENCES Aloud!

Quotation Marks (" ") are used to express a direct quote, to enclose slang and technical terms. Use an open quote mark(") at the beginning of the quote and a closed quote mark (") at the end. Quotation marks are also used to enclose titles of poems, stories, essays, articles, chapters of books, songs, and radio and television programs.

> Jeff said to me, "I knew you were up to something."
> My favorite song is, "America The Beautiful."

Punctuation that refers to the quote stays **inside** the quotation mark. Remember that quotation marks are used to enclose the actual words of the character and the punctuation.

Inside: John said, "Who saw the kitten last?"

> The Mechanics of Writing help keep your story Fine Tuned!

Computer users please note: When you begin a quote, (since there is only one quote mark on the keyboard), do the following: **Shift**" to type the first quote mark, then type, (no space) and at the end of the quote: **Shift**" (no space after last letter). You can see the beginning and end quote marks fall in the proper directions. (If you don't use this procedure or if you leave a space between the quote and the first or last letter, the marks will be in the wrong direction).

Single Quotation Marks (' ') are used to enclose a quote within a quote.
"I heard John say, 'Be sure you get home by six'."

Apostrophe (') expresses the <u>possessive</u> forms of most nouns/pronouns.
Singular: girl's gloves —
Plural ends in s, the ' follows the s: girls' gloves.
If the plural noun doesn't end in *s*, such as men, add an apostrophe and *s*:men's.
The apostrophe is also used in contractions, to show that letters have been omitted and for personal possession. Here are 2 examples:
He couldn't believe how big the mountain was. (contraction)
Tom's book is fascinating.   (possession)

Colon (:) is used before a list, to identify the speaker in plays and scripts, and before a formal statement.
(list) My mom told me to pick up three items:
soap, shampoo, and toothpaste.
(identify the speaker) Juliet: Romeo, where
fore art thou Romeo?
(formal statement)   The agreement states: We
will abide by these
terms.

Semicolon (;) is used to separate parts of a list and as a more pronounced break in long sentences. It can also be used between incomplete sentences that are not joined by a conjunction (and, but, or, etc.) or by a conjunction adverb (however, indeed, etc.). Think of the semicolon as more than a comma and less than a period.
My birthday is June 29; Mary's is September 7.
We thought the band was entertaining; others thought the show was boring.
Our costs were: tires, $25; fuel $50; oil $20.25.

Hyphen (-) is used to designate a continuation of a word that has been divided at the end of a line. When used to continue a word, one-syllable words should not be divided, and multi-syllabic words should be divided between syllables.

> Evie regretted not knowing the modeling job was like walking into Con-troller's evil web. If she had though about it she wouldn't have gone.
> My lunch break is usually around a half-hour.

Dash (--) is used to indicate an abrupt change of thought or flow in the sentence.   It is also used to introduce a phrase that summarizes the rest of the statement. (use only 2)

> The three P's --)planning, preparing and persisting -- are the
> keys to success.
> Respect, good teamwork, a love of the game -- these are the qualities
> that make champions.

Parentheses [( )] enclose extra information, or description, that's not relevant enough to the sentence to require a comma. Sentences that contain parentheses should read as well without them as they do with them.

> John's cat (the brown one) likes catnip.
> I added salt (sea salt) to the recipe.

Ellipsis (...) omission of a word or words necessary for a complete construction of the sentences but understood. The dots (...) form a punctuation mark indicating the omission of a word or words or change of thought, but understood by the reader (3 periods)

> There is something more to do ... but that can wait.

.... or periods are used when the omission comes at the end of a sentence. (4 periods)

> This is all we have to say....

Punctuation and Writing Dialogue

Punctuation can be tricky when you write dialogue. Dialogue should reflect the spoken words as closely as possible. When writing dialogue, indent five spaces (as a paragraph) for each line spoken by a character.

> See example of spaces (_____) = 's 5 spaces
>> Two friends meet at a restaurant to discuss a problem one of the women is
>> having.
>> _____ "John works late every night," Myra said as she sipped her coffee.
>> _____ "Have you told him how disappointed you are when he doesn't
>> come home for dinner?"

You can see how indenting makes dialogue easier to read. Also, notice how this conversation flows without repeating "she said" tags after each character speaks? Tags are often necessary to show which character is speaking, but don't overwork them.   Instead use description.

Colons and Semi-colons Within Dialogue
Generally, colons or semicolons are not used within dialogue.

> Greg wanted to go to Stonebrook College; his father insisted he try West Point first.

But in dialogue you'd write:

> Greg said, "I want to go to Stonebrook College!"
> His father insisted, "Greg you will go to West Point first."

The Dash and The Ellipses In Dialogue
You can use the dash to punctuate a line of dialogue interrupted by an action

> "You played very well, Sally" - - she waved her hand - - "I'll see you later."

You can use the ellipsis to show speech that trails off.

> "If you don't come out of the pool this instant, I'll . . . .

Numbers In Dialogue
Spell out numbers in dialogue.

> "He'll be here at two-thirty," Joyce announced.

For dates and other long numbers it is acceptable to use numerals.

> "The license number on the new car is 13882," the police officer said.

Writing Numbers
When writing numbers, it's easy to make mistakes. As a general rule, numbers 10 and under are spelled out;

> My three brothers are on the baseball team,

Spell out numbers one through ten, except when there is a series of related numbers.

> The girls sold 2 boxes of cookies, 3 dozen candy bars, and 16 bags of popcorn.

Use numerals for numbers over 10

> More than 300 people attended the conference.

Always write out numbers at the beginning of a sentence.

> Three hundred and twenty-five shirts were packed.

Or don't start a sentence with a number

> We packed 325 shirts.

Always spell out numbers at the beginning of sentences even when other numbers are present.

> Fifteen children, 10 boys and 5 girls, were in the class.

Writing styles vary, and writing numbers for a statistical report would differ from a less statistical one. When many numbers are needed, use numerals:

> By March 3, 1999, more than 17 stores closed. A survey revealed that only 10 had moved to other locations and 7 had filed bankruptcy.

In less statistical writing, follow these basic rules:

> Three years ago, Marge decided to sell seventy acres of her thousand-acre farm. She closed the deal in January, 2001.

Numbers in the thousands, millions and above are generally spelled out.
Old Paul claims that over the years he has saved over two million dollars.

If you want to Practice Writing Numbers STOP on the side of the road and Review the routes. Decide whether the correct answer is the numeral or the word.

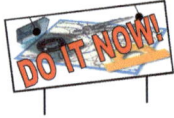

She owns _____cats. Fill in a number up to 10

There were _____ players. Fill in a number above 10

The boy's were age _____, _____ and _____
Fill in two numbers below 10 and one above 10

Paul owes over _____.
Fill in number above thousands

SEE Answers Upside Down

Corrected Sentences and Explanations

She owns at least *five* cats. (Numbers 10 and under are generally spelled out)

2. There were *35* players. (Numbers above 10 are generally written as numerals)

3. The boy's ages are *3, 8,* and *17*. (Numbers under 10 are written as numerals when there is a series of related numbers)

4. Paul owes over *two million* dollars. (Numbers in the thousands, millions and above are generally spelled out)

Frequently Misspelled Words

It's easy to misspell words because so many words sound alike, but nothing makes a work look amateurish as much as misspelled words. Misspelled words should be rare, if at all. Use a Dictionary. Now you ask if I don't know how to spell, how do I look up the word to spell. Suppose you're unsure about the word vacuum. When you say the word you think...

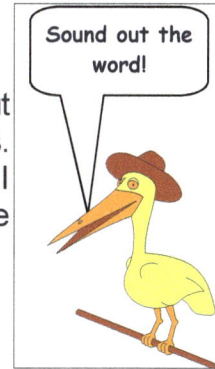

V A Q U M

Begin to look up as many letters as possible in the dictionary that have these letters — Start with Va next try and look for the "q" sound. If q is not the next letter try a similar sounding letter — c or k. And, so on, until you find the word vacuum. (see below)

va·cu·i·ty (vækjú:iti:) *pl.* va·cu·i·ties *n.* the state or quality of being vacuous ‖ something pointless [fr. L. *vacuitas*]

vac·u·o·late (vækju:ouleit) *adj.* vacuolated vác·u·o·lat·ed *adj.* containing vacuoles

vac·u·ole (vækju:oul) *n.* (*biol.*) a minute cavity in cell protoplasm containing air, sap or partly digested food ‖ a small cavity in organic tissue [F.]

vac·u·ous (vækju:əs) *adj.* having or showing a lack of understanding or intelligence or serious purpose ‖ emptied of content (e.g. of air or gas) [fr. L. *vacuus*, empty]

vac·u·um (vækju:əm, vækju:m) 1. *pl.* vac·u·ums, vac·u·a (vækju:ə) *n.* a part of space in which no matter exists ‖ a space largely exhausted of air ‖ space containing air or gas at a pressure below that of the atmosphere ‖ (*pl.* vacuums) a void, *her departure left a vacuum* ‖ (*pl.* vacuums) a vacuum cleaner 2. *v.t.* to clean with a vacuum cleaner [L. neut. of *vacuus*, empty]
—Aristotle insisted that a vacuum was an impossibility, using this argument to explain the cohesion of a solid, and this dogma persisted for

Then read the definition to be sure you have gotten the right word. When working on a computer use Spell Check. (Note: When a word can be spelled differently depending on the definition, you need to be extra careful to use the correct spelling. Such as to, too and two, or there and their. The computer might show the word as spelled   correctly, but **Our Guides Suggest** you also run a Grammar Check which might highlight the Error. The best answer is to read your work carefully. We also suggest using a professional editor to be sure your work is presented professionally to a publisher.

For   more   information   about   editing   visit   our   website   at: www.goldenquillpress.com

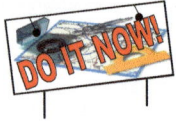

Get your Writing Map 8 **MISSPELLED WORDS** Form
from your Travel Kit at the back of this chapter
And review the most popular misspelled words.
**Use this page and next to keep track of your
most often misspelled words**

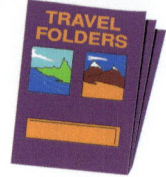

USE THIS AND THE NEXT PAGE

Writing Map 8

Writing Map 8

TRIP REVIEW

Map Directions

Whatever Vehicle You Use, Don't Forget The Mechanics Of Writing

Use The Mechanics Technical Manual As A Reference When Writing

Punctuation Helps Your Characters Speak For You

Travel Instructions — Did You?

- ☐☐ Review your Technical Manual
- ☐☐ Add your Misspelled Words to
- ☐☐ Update your Reference Library

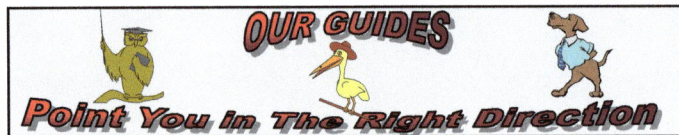

OUR GUIDES

Point You in The Right Direction

WISE Guides Write Right Punctuation and Spelling

Friend: Misspelled "Frend" made me a Fiend

This dog wants "1,0000000" or is it "one million bones"

◄ **NOTE** ►
Too much punctuation is as confusing as too little.

Writing Map 8

COMMONLY MISSPLELLED WORDS

Travel Kit Form

acknowledgment	forge	professor
advertisement	friend	quandary
agreement	gauge	receipt
analysis	grateful	receive
anniversary	hoping	reference
apologize	hypocrisy	renown
arctic	independent	respectfully
asinine	ingenious	restaurateur
background	innate	sentence
balloon	inoculate	separate
bastion	judgment	sincerely
battalion	liaison	sophomore
bookkeeper	liquefy	subtly
business	lose	superintendent
ceiling	marshmallow	supersede
cemetery	minuscule	threshold
complexion	moccasin	tragedy
controversy	owing	truly
correspondent	pastime	until
disagreeable	pharaoh	
dissipate	poinsettia	
fluorescent	proceed	

ADD YOUR FREQUENTLY MISSPELLED WORDS

_____	_____	_____
_____	_____	_____
_____	_____	_____
_____	_____	_____
_____	_____	_____
_____	_____	_____
_____	_____	_____
_____	_____	_____

Writing Map 9

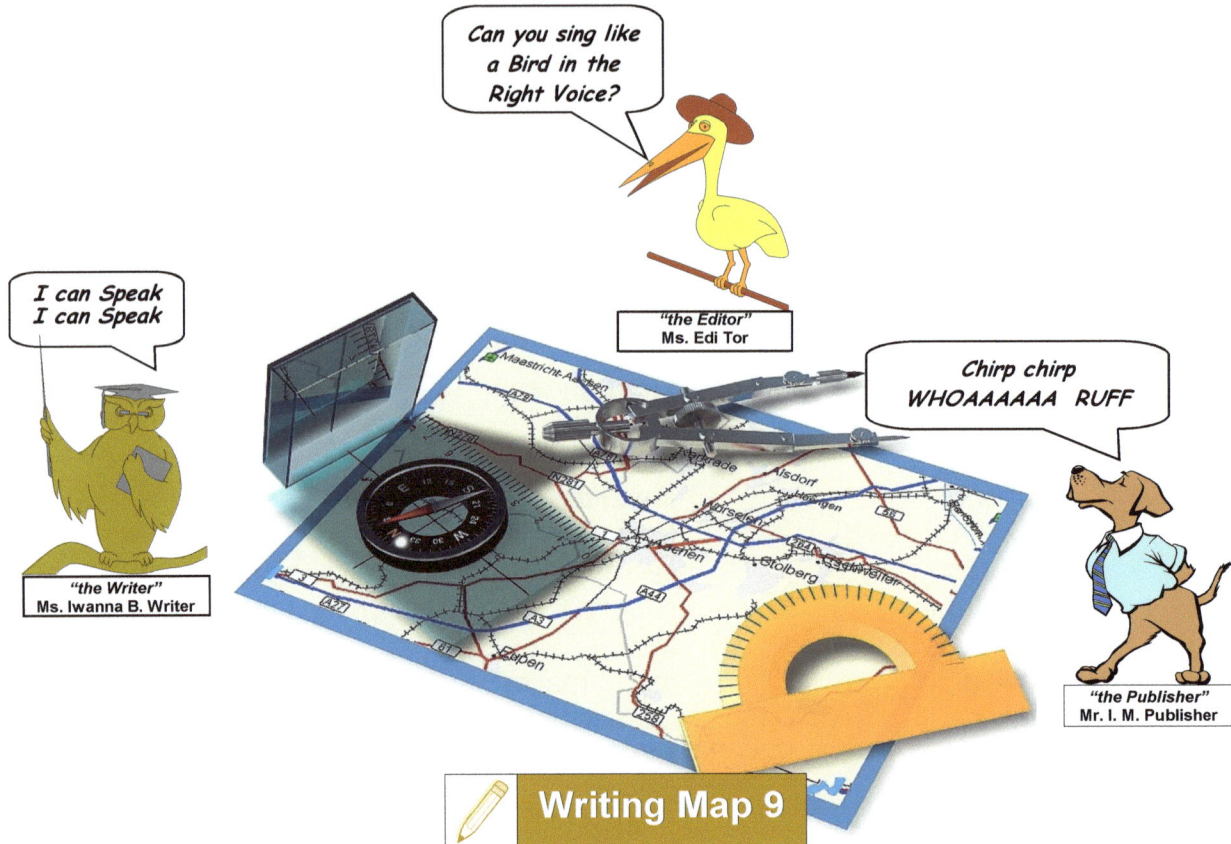

CHARACTER'S SPEAK UP

As a writer your words bring your story to life. Giving your characters the right voice is important; it's how they speak. You give your characters voice by use of vocabulary; choosing the right words, and then creating tone by how you handle dialogue. A character who is 80 years old, obviously, would not speak in the same voice as a child, or a young person.

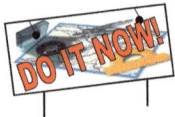

Take the following situation and see if you can pick out who's saying what

Four people: a three year old boy, an elderly woman, a businessman, and a young mother, all have the same experience. Each stumbled on a piece of broken concrete on a sidewalk. Their dialogue should identify which of these people is speaking:

1. "Ouch! I fall down and hurt my toe." _____

2. "Why can't this city repair these sidewalks? We pay enough taxes!" _____

3. "Oh, my, I didn't even see that hole in the sidewalk. I could've fallen and broken my hip!" _____

4. "Someone's child is going to fall down and get hurt."_____

15

SEE ANSWERS UPSIDE DOWN

Identity Clues - Would the mother say" "Ouch! I fall down ?

Read the sentences again to see how the choice of words and punctuation helps you set the tone in dialogue.

Creating Realistic Dialogue

You may read a story with little or no dialogue, yet the narrator has made it so interesting and compelling that you know how your characters are relating and communicating. However, in most stories, authors have their characters talking. They balance description and dialogue to move the story along.

You may be able to paint fascinating word pictures, such as describing the many colors of a rainbow at sunset, but be aware of overworking description. Today's readers like action and dialogue — a fast read!

Dialogue can be used to create tension, heighten suspense and to intensify conflicts. Dialogue can reveal a character's inner emotions, goals and motivations. Dialogue is also used effectively as a devise for pacing a story.

Tension and Conflict

Example: Mary was not in the mood to sit at home night after night.
   "I'm not going out, I'm tired after a days work." Tom said.
   "Well! I'm not cooking dinner. I sit home all day and I need to get out of this house. I'm going whether you come with me or not!" Mary grabbed her coat and handbag.
   "You can open a can of beans," she shouted as she slammed the door behind her.

There's so much tension I can't speak - ugh--edit

This scene shows tension and conflict in conversation. If you wrote this scene without dialogue, would you be able to visualize the tension and conflict expressed by the characters, Mary and Tom?

Dialogue and Setting

Example: The Kanes were relocating to Island Falls and looking for a new home.
   "There it is, Mom!" Evie said. "That white Colonial with the pillars and green shutters. Dad, pull into the driveway." Evie was bubbling with excitement.
   "Look, it has a three car garage," Martin laughed, "Room enough for my workshop."
"And the landscaping must have cost a fortune—the backyard has a flower garden, too." Vivian had dreamed of having more than a few potted plants on a window sill. "I can't wait to see it."

Does the dialogue help you visualize the house? Could you portray the emotions felt by The Kanes without the dialogue?

Get your Writing Map 9 **DIALOGUE DETAILING** Form
from your Travel Kit at the back of this chapter

When you feel your story is becoming bogged down, you can use dialogue to speed up action. If the story is moving at a faster pace than it should, you can slow it down by having you character engage in conversation or thoughts that seem natural.

> Rebecca had waited until her husband finished his coffee before she spoke. "Cal, I'm so sorry, but ...I'm leaving you."
> Cal paused to collect his thoughts before speaking. After a long silence, he looked up at Rebecca, "Why has it taken you so long to speak up?"
> Rebecca avoided looking at her husband of 30 years as she tried to think of how she could explain why she was leaving him.

You can see how this dialogue has slowed the pace by using words such as: paused, long silence, avoided and waited. Faster pace words might include: hurry, excited, interrupted. When using dialogue to control pacing, choose words that reflect what your characters are experiencing.

List 5 words that Slow the Pace and 5 Words that Speed Up the Pace

_____   _____   _____   _____   _____

_____   _____   _____   _____   _____

Use the Active Voice

The way you write a sentence and your choice of words can make your writing dull or give it color and dynamic impact. When you write in the passive voice, you tend to become wordy and your writing loses its quality and effectiveness. The active voice is less wordy and has a more positive tone.

> Passive: The car was driven home by Helen.
> Active: Helen drove the car home.

> Passive and wordy: It was agreed that John should be recommended
>   to our publisher and this has been done.
> Active and concise: We all agreed to recommend John to our publisher.

Change the following to the active voice:
> Passive: A house is being built by John Smith.

Active: _____

> Passive: In the yard the children are playing.

Active: _____

SEE ANSWERS UPSIDE DOWN

Answers: 1. John Smith is building a house. - 2. Children are playing in the yard.

Nouns and Pronouns – Person, Place or Thing

> HE, SHE, IT or I.M, IWANNA, and...

When writing about a specific person, avoid over-working pronouns "he" or "she."

> **Example:** John began **his** new job after **he** moved to California. **He** enjoyed working with **his** colleagues and **he** soon became leader of **his** team. **He** soon moved up in the company, where **he** became Ace Company's youngest Editor.

You can see how the pronoun "he" has been overworked. Note the difference when the paragraph is written "tighter."

> **Example:** John began a new job after moving to California. **He** enjoyed working with **his** new colleagues and soon became the team leader. John is Ace Company's youngest Editor.

On the other hand, it can become boring to the reader when you eliminate all pronouns and always use the noun.

> **Example: Sara** was going shopping. **Sara** drove to town where **Sara** met her friend. **Sara** called her mother to tell her she would be late.

Here's a better version:

> **Sara** was going shopping. **She** drove to town to meet her friend for lunch. **Sara** called to tell her mother to tell her she would be late.

The careful use of nouns and pronouns helps the reader visualize and identify characters as your story progresses.

Verbs: Action Words--Past, Present and Future

The verb expresses action; a condition or state of being. When writing a story, it's easy to get caught up in telling the story and forget to watch verb tenses. The reader needs to have an understanding of when an action is taking place. When writing, be sure to check verb tenses as you progress.

Principal Parts of Verbs

Present	Past	Past Participle	Future
Break	Broke	Broken	Break
Choose	Chose	Chosen	Choose
Do	Did	Done	Do
Drive	Drove	Driven	Drive
Know	Knew	Known	Know
Speak	Spoke	Spoken	Speak

 Write the present, past, past participle and future of the word "write"

_____   _____   _____   _____

SEE ANSWERS UPSIDE DOWN

Answers: Write   wrote   written   write

> You can't always say do, did, done, do... sometimes you need FUTURE Perfect Tense—will be

19

Additional Review of Verb Tenses

Tense	Use	Example
Present	to show what is happening now	I **write** stories.
Past	to show what happened at a time in the past	I **wrote** poetry when I was young.
Future	to show what will happen in the future	I may try to **write** a novel some day.
Present Perfect	happened in the past and continues in the present	I **have written** from my garden for years and I like **writing** there.
Past Perfect	happened in the past even before another action or event	The book **was written** before the editor approved it.
Future Perfect	something that has not yet happened, but will before some time in the future	By Monday the instructor **will have written** all the lessons for the week.
Present Continuous	an event that is happening now	I **am writing** new stories everyday.
Past Continuous	to show an event happening when something else happens	I **was writing** when my computer crashed
Future Continuous	something will happen when something else takes place	The author **will have written** the ending before finishing the manuscript.

Adjectives and Adverbs

Overworking adjectives and adverbs can clutter your writing with pretentious wordiness.
Adjectives - Describe or identify nouns and pronouns, (person, place or thing).
      This cake is delicious
      The adjective *delicious* describes the noun *cake*.

Adverbs - Describe verbs, (action words) and other adverbs. Adverbs answer the question of when, where, how, to what degree or extent.
      When: We saw her an hour ago.
      Where: We marched onward.
      How: He spoke glowingly
      Extent: She could hardly hear me.

Words can often be over-worked— Exceedingly – Really – Very -- Hopefully – That
Here are A Few and Our Suggestions:
      Overworked —The weather was exceedingly pleasant.
          The weather was pleasant.
      Overworked — He really likes baseball.
          He likes baseball.
      Overworked — The cake is very good.
          The cake is delicious.
      Overworked — We will hopefully get there in time.
          We hope to get there in time.
      Overworked — People think that dogs are fun pets.
          People think dogs are fun pets.

Dialogue Tags – License Plates for Dialogue

   Tags have one purpose in dialogue — to identify the speaker. Common examples of tags are "he said," or "she said." When tags are used after every line of dialogue, they detract from the imagery you're trying to create for the reader.

> "I'm going to work, see you tonight" he said.
>
> "When you come home we can discuss dinner," she said, hoping he would suggest going out for their anniversary.

This conversation is dull and boring. You don't need to use "said" in every line. Description can create a better and more natural flow.

> "I'm going to work," Bob called out as he picked up his car keys and headed for the garage.
>
> "Do you want to have dinner at home or shall I meet you somewhere?" Jan responded, trying not to show how disappointed she was. Bob had forgotten their anniversary.
>
> "I'm in the garage, and can't hear you." Bob snickered to himself. Looking at her anniversary present; a new car. He opened the door and suggested, "Can you come out here. I want to show you something."

We've used descriptive action to replace he said, she said. Telling what the character is doing makes your dialogue more interesting and moves your story along better at the same time. When writing dialogue, weigh each word carefully for meaning and remember an occasional "he said" "she said" works too.

Writing Dialogue

   At times, tags, such as, "He said" or "She said" may be all you need to make your characters and scenes come alive.

When you feel you need more colorful and descriptive words, refer to Your Travel Folder Map 9 TAG LIST Form for ideas and add words you can use instead of said.

Get your Writing Map 9 **TAG LIST** Form
from your Travel Kit at the back of this chapter

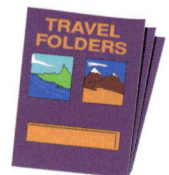

Create a story without "he said, she said." Experiment with words that will adjust the pacing; slower and faster. NOTE: When 2 people are speaking you do not need to identify the speaker, unless the dialogue is getting very long. When several people are speaking you must identify who is speaking to keep it clear for the reader.

Add your suggestions for replacing "he said" "she said"
e - mail: info@goldenquillpress.com

Using the Best Meaning

Use words to express what you mean as you paint word-pictures for your reader. A sentence can fall flat or it can create strong imagery, purely by your choice of words. Stronger words leap off the page:

Strong Action Words: Choose which expression you would use:
Mary is annoyed and expresses her emotion by:
Closing the door behind her.
Slamming the door behind her.
Shutting the door behind her.

_____

Correct Answer:
Mary would **slam** the door because if she is annoyed she's more likely to express her emotion with the stronger action.

Using Formal and Informal Words

Just as you dress appropriately for different occasions, you need to choose the right words for the kind of piece you're writing. At times the more formal word works — other times the simple word works better.

formal -- He will ascertain if the document is legal.
simple -- He will find out if the document is legal.

Formal	Informal
deceased	dead, passed away
endeavor	try
facilitate	make easy
in lieu of	instead
residence	home
sufficient	enough
terminate	end, stop
transpire	happen

Rhythm and Flow

Reading your work aloud and tapping (like a drummer), you can hear the rhythm and flow. You can also tape yourself and check the playback. There's no set rule for sentence length, but be cautious when your sentences seem too long or too short. When sentence after sentence is short and choppy, your writing becomes monotonous.
Example: Johnny ran home from school. He wanted to see his grandmother. She was coming to visit. She always brought lots of presents.

Running sentences on and on without punctuation can be just as annoying as short choppy ones.

> **Example:** Johnny ran all the way home from school because he couldn't wait to see his grandmother who was coming to visit and Johnny knew she would be bringing lots of presents and he was happy.

Whew! When a sentence runs 20 to 30 words or more, dissect it to see where you can use punctuation.

> **Example:** Johnny ran all the way home from school. He couldn't wait to see his grandmother who was coming to visit. He was happy because he knew she'd be bringing presents.

Tightening the Seat Belts

Cut out excess words, paragraphs, even chapters that are not relevant. Follow these detours and tighten up.

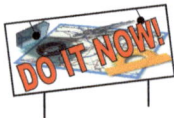

 Fix these overly wordy sentences

1. Wordy: When you have finished your work, you can then go home.

_____

2. Wordy: That was the very same cat that I saw jumping on the chair.

_____

SEE ANSWERS UPSIDE DOWN

Answers: 1. Better: When you finish your work, go home. 2. Better: That's the cat I saw on the chair.

The Right Word Turning Signal

The English Language contains many words that are similar in either sound, or meaning. When aren't sure which word is right - look it up.

 Get your Writing Map 9 **RIGHT WORDS** Form from your Travel Kit at the back of this chapter

Use this list often when writing to be sure you
Write the Right Word for Your Right Meaning!

✏️ Writing Map 9

TRIP REVIEW

Map Directions

Dialogue: Controls Pacing, Creates Tension, Heightens Suspense & Intensifies Conflict

Dialogue Gives the Reader Personal Involvement In Your Story

Description Is important, But Dialogue Moves The Story Along

Travel Instructions — Did You?

❑ Scout for License Plate Tags to use instead of "He Said," "She Said"

❑ Watch your Detours and places to pay attention to "The Right Words"

❑ Add Writing Map 9 Forms to your 🧳

OUR GUIDES
Point You In The Right Direction

Formal; or Informal.
Let Who's Speaking
Decide

Read Dialogue Aloud to
be sure Your Characters
Sound True to Life

Active Voices Barking
Well Paced Dialogue
–A Great Read

◄ NOTE ►

Dialogue is the means by which your characters communicate.

Writing Map 9 — DIALOGUE DETAILING — Form

EXAMPLE: Dialogue Detailing

Just then, Jonathan and Rick came busting through the door. "We came to make the odds more even," Jonathan boasted.

"You are late for this exam." Quiz Master shouted at the two boys. "If you do not find your seats in one minute, your will both be marked absent and will: A. Fail, B. Fail or, C. Cause Brad here to have a very nasty accident.

Jonathan and Rick quickly found crates and sat down.

Quiz Master then informed them, "Now, you boys did not do your homework, or you would have known that when you opened the door, you tripped an electronic devise," the hologram laughed. "The common term, for your edification, might be: A. bomb, B. false alarm, C. electrical explosive or D. booby trap or not .... This is of course multiple choice, but which ever you choose, A, B, C or D the timer is counting down the destruction of this warehouse as we speak. Oh such fun," the hologram danced around, "this is turning out to be an incredible lesson. Everything and everyone will be destroyed. That is, of course, except me!"

Phoenix wanted to get everyone out of the warehouse to safety, but without knowing what other disasters might be triggered, he did not dare. He signaled Dove who was keeping an eye on a very distraught Sheila. "What about me?" Sheila moved away from Brad and positioned herself between Quiz Master and the class.

"Sorry my dear, the casualties of being in this class, you know! You are expendable along with your other classmates. Sometimes it is necessary to make a point so everyone can learn, and if you must go too... ah well!"

Dialogue Detailing:

_____
_____
_____
_____
_____
_____
_____
_____
_____
_____
_____
_____
_____
_____
_____
_____
_____
_____
_____
_____
_____
_____
_____
_____
_____
_____
_____
_____
_____
_____

Writing Map 9 TAG WORDS **Form**

A
added
agreed
answered
asked

B
barked
bellowed
blurted
boasted
bubbled

C
commanded
commented
complained
continued

D
declared
defended
demanded
directed
drawled

E
emphasized
exclaimed
explained
exploded

G
gasped
giggled
grinned
groaned
grumbled

H
hissed
hollered
howled
hummed

I
insisted
interrupted
invited

J
joked

L
laughed

M
moaned
muttered

O
ordered

P
persisted
pleaded
protested

Q
quipped

R
recalled
related
replied
responded
roared

S
said
scoffed
scolded
shouted
sighed
snapped
snickered
snorted
spoke
sputtered
stammered
stated
suggested

T
teased
thought

U
urged

W
whimpered
whined
whispered
wondered

Y
yelped

ADD YOUR OWN TAG WORDS

_____   _____   _____

_____   _____   _____

_____   _____   _____

_____   _____   _____

Writing Map 9

USING THE RIGHT WORD

Form

Affect/Effect
Affect means to influence.
Her unhappiness affected us.
Effect means to accomplish;
The effect will be known soon.

Amount/Number
Amount- bulk quantities
They dumped a large amount of soil on the street.
Number - countable quantities
There were a number of birds on the lawn.

Bad/Badly
Bad - not good
This is a bad apple.
Badly - poorly done or felt
The work was badly done.

Can/May
Can - ability to do something
I can go to school today.
May - permission to do something
You may go to the movies.

Cheap/Inexpensive
Cheap - implies shoddiness
Cheap fabric won't wear well.
Inexpensive - less costly
Inexpensive fabrics will last.

Distrust/Mistrust
Distrust- lack of faith, suspicion
I have reason to distrust him.
Mistrust – lack of confidence
I mistrust what the ad claims.

Feasible/Possible
Feasible - practical
That is a feasible plan.
Possible - able to be done
It is possible to solve this.

Few/Less
Few - things counted
I have fewer days to work .
Less - things measured in other ways
We used less water today.

Foreword/Forward
Foreword - comment at the beginning of a book
I will write the foreword to the book.
Forward - movement toward a point in time or space
Move the chair forward.

Further/Farther
Further - refers to time
Further along in the project we'll have more time.
Farther - refers to distance
The house is farther down the street.

Irregardless
DO NOT USE THIS WORD
Instead Use regardless:
We will progress regardless of obstacles in our way.

Its/It's
Its - possessive form of it
The bee stored its honey.
It's - contraction of it is
It's time to go.

Lay/Lie
Lay - to put something in place
Lay the books on the table.
Lie - to repose
You should lie down.

Like/Such as
Like - similar
This doll is like yours.
Such As - used when referring to specific persons, places, or things
Houses such as these are rare.

May/Might
These two words are interchangeable, but might connotes slightly more uncertainty than may
You might want to eat lunch early.
You may want to eat lunch early.

Me/I
NOTE: Very Easy To Confuse so do the test: Where are You?
HINT: Reverse the answer such as:
Me am here or I am here
Or make it singular
Go with John and me. Go with John and I.
HINT: Take off John and see.
Go with me. or Go with I.
Of course me is correct.

Site/Cite
Site - location
They will build on this site.
Cite - to call attention to
We will cite him for bravery.

This/That
This - something close by
This is my coat.
That - something more remote in distance or time
I intend to buy that coat next week.

Who/Whom
(Whom is the objective form of who).
Jan, whom I spoke with earlier today, called back.
I don't know who lives next door.

Your/You're
Your means belonging to you.
It is your book.
You're – contraction of you are
You're the best friend I have.

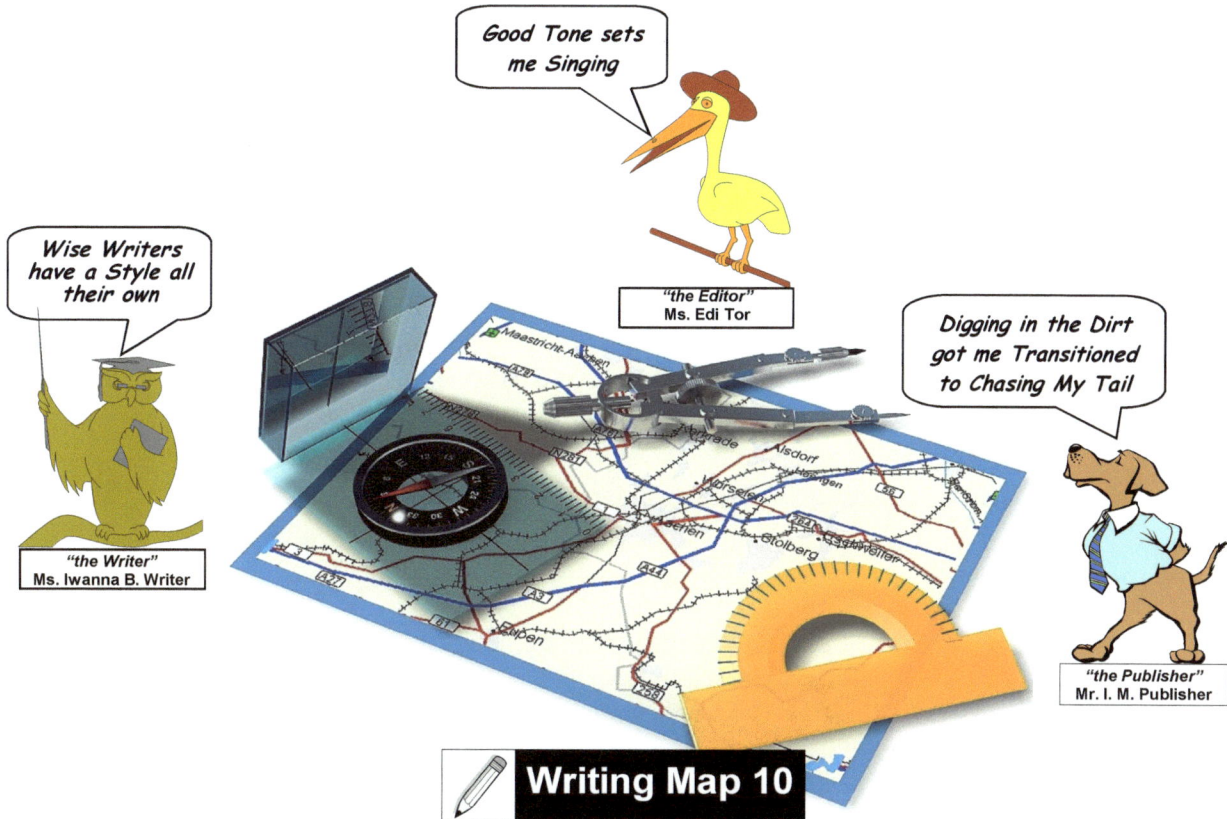

YOUR WRITING STYLE

You're not born with a writing style, it's something you develop as you begin to write. Your style is your manner of expressing your ideas and thoughts; distinct from other writers.

Writers have been known to try to imitate the writing styles of famous writers such as Jane Austin, Pearl Buck, Charles Dickens, Ernest Hemingway or others whose books continue to sell year after year; or modern writers, such as: Clancy, Grisham, King and Steele. What imitators fail to realize is that a painting by Picasso differs from a Van Gogh. The same is true for writing styles. Your writing style uses language that expresses your visions so your reader hears, sees, feels, and senses not only the magic of your words, but all the meanings they convey.

Take Your Style via the Highway of Emotion in Tone

When you speak, your voice has a tone that expresses emotion and enhances the meaning of your words. You use a different tone of voice to express anger than to express joy. When writing, your choice of words and how you punctuate sentences helps convey the mood you want to set. Tone is the overall mood you establish in your writing to make your story come alive on the page, and it's a valuable tool when writing dialogue.

Read the following sentences aloud to see how punctuation and word choice can change the tone and mood of the same sentence.

"I'm going to work," she said.
"Going to work?" she asked.
"I'm going to work!" she shouted.
"I'm just going to work." she explained.

DO IT NOW! Practice writing for tone. You've lost a favorite item or a large sum of money. Express your disappointment in two sentences. Give the first sentence a little emotion and the second express everything you're feeling. Read your sentences aloud, and see if you have written the emotions into the tone.

_____

_____

_____

Turn onto the Highway of Tone via Description

Tone in writing is not limited to dialogue. You can set the tone (and mood) by the words you use to describe just about anything. If you wrote, "It was a dark and stormy night," this opening line sets a tone by describing the weather.

In contrast, you might write, "It was a bright, sunny day in spring. Birds were singing and flowers were blooming." These sentences set the opposite tone.

You can see that consistency is important. If you were to write: "It was dark and stormy and the birds were singing," it would be confusing. But, if you said the sunny day turned into a dark and stormy night, that would be a good lead in for a change in tone.

It's important to keep the tone of your writing consistent and to be careful when you change the tone.

> The baby was laughing as his mother sang to him, then all of a sudden, he began to cry. She held him on her shoulder, patting his tiny back. "Go to sleep," she cooed, but the baby cried louder. Suddenly, she felt the tiny body stiffen. Her baby was choking—turning blue. Holding the struggling child with one arm, she raced to the telephone and dialed 911.

Mixing tone comes out all chirped up--

This short scene shows how tone can change within a scene. Here, the scene begins with a happy tone, then changes to one of fear and anxiety. If you were to write this story from beginning to end, the under-tone would be the mother's love and concern for her child.

Finish this story and change the tone back to joy as the baby's life is saved. Use your description and dialogue to show anxiety and fear turning to relief and happiness.

_____

_____

Transitioning from one road to the next—Use the Bridge!

Transitions are the bridges you use to get from one thought to the next. They are the connecting roads that lead the reader from one paragraph to another and one chapter to another. Transitions are necessary to keep advancing your story in a natural flow. Without transitions your main theme can get lost, especially in a long article or novel. In movies, transitions occur as a scene ends and is then picked up again, at another time or place. When writing a story, transitions help you manage dates and time; move your characters from place to place and help you avoid having to write out every small detail.

The Time Transition Technique

This short example uses time transitions to move the story along. Visualize Annie and what has happened in her life, past, present, and what she sees for the future.

Every day began at dawn for Annie. She had to care for the farm animals, cook; do all the household chores, and keep the books for the thousand-acre farm where she lived with her father. (This paragraph introduces the character in the present time. The following paragraph is the transition to the past)

Annie's mother had died five years ago, in a tragic accident. Her mother had gone to take her father his lunch. As she ran beside the tractor to hand the lunchbox up to him, the machine swerved, striking Annie's mother. Annie's father blamed himself for the death of his wife and over the years he had changed into a bitter, fault-finding old man. (Now the transition will bring the character back to the present and shows the effect of the past.)

Annie tried to talk about her mother with her father, but he refused any conversation, so Annie did her chores during the week and planned outings to get her out of the house on Saturdays. This Saturday she would do her shopping, then meet Danny Roberts at the ice cream store. Her heart was breaking. His father had gotten a new job and his family would be moving to California. Someone else she loved would be leaving her life. (The following paragraph sets up another transition. Now we are stating the present time.)

Saturday morning, Annie happily started down the stairs, but her father was waiting with the car keys in hand. "I'm driving into town today," he growled. "There's not gonna be a trip to the ice cream store for you Missy Anne, so don't think you're gonna see that Robert's boy. Not today and thankfully, not ever again."

During the two-mile trip into town, Annie fought back the tears. She had to get to Danny!

DO IT NOW! Practice writing transitions, continue the story by finishing what happens when Annie and her father get to town?

_____

_____

_____

_____

_____

There are many different ways to use transitions. They can be used from one paragraph to another; one sentence to another or even within a sentence. They are very important when moving from one chapter to another. Transitions should be brief and inconspicuous in your writing.

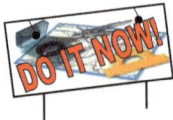

DO IT NOW! Get your Writing Map 10 **BRIDGES TO TRANSITION** Form from your Travel Kit at the back of this chapter.
Review words and phrases that help make transitions

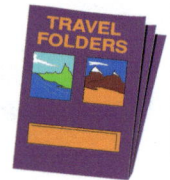

Use this form to add words and phrases you would use to take your characters from one place to another, from one time to another and from one Chapter to another.

ALERT:
Our Wise Guides Agree:
Transitions are essential to keep your reader from asking—

Didn't he have on a blue tie?

Wasn't he in the kitchen? How did he get in the car?

Wasn't he born in New York in 1960? But this is 1700

Metaphor and Imagery

A metaphor is a figure of speech containing an implied comparison of two things. Often, writers use metaphors to compare feelings to something different, such as an object or action. If you just wanted to show feeling you could write, "She looked sad and began to cry." But when you use a metaphor you can show the feelings as compared to a gray stormy day.

Example: Her face clouded over as the tears rained down her cheeks.
The gloom of the day had settled on her face.
The metaphor combines two ideas that become somewhat the same.

Example: Black velvet curtains of night enfolded the village.
We can visualize the night resembling the curtains as they are closed for the evening

Example: Silver ribbons of water flowed down the mountain.
We visualize water flowing down the mountain in a narrow ribbon.

   In the metaphor examples: the storm, curtains, ribbons all add imagery (pictures in the mind) to express the thoughts in a different, but often more powerful manner. Memorable people, places, and experiences, are enhanced by the use of imagery.

DO IT NOW!   Get your Writing Map 10 **METAPHOR, IMAGERY,**
SIMILE DETAILING FORM at the back of this chapter.
Decide on one main location - Repeat for additional locations   TRAVEL FOLDERS

Simile

   Simile means likeness or having a resemblance to something.
       The man is strong as an elephant.
       The man's wrinkled gray skin hung on his bony frame, like an elephant's hide.
You can use metaphors, imagery and similes in your writing to create vivid impressions, that can be interwoven into your story in a subtle manner.   They should not appear to be contrived.
Use the form to write your scene adding similes and metaphors to create vivid imagery and use this to add to your scene descriptions.

Turn Right at the Clichés

   The word "cliché" means a tired, worn-out, trite expression. Overworked words and phrases can make your writing dull and lacking in freshness and originality.

DO IT NOW! Change THESE Clichés into better phrases, such as: Music to my ears becomes -- That sounds really great!

As luck would have it   _____

Trapped like rats   _____

Cool as a cucumber   _____

Goes without saying _____

Water over the dam _____

See answers upside down

1.The way it turned out 2.Cornered 3.Easy going 4.Words aren't needed 5. As if it never happened

Stereotyping

An example of stereotyping can be seen in movies where all the good cowboys wear white hats and the bad ones wear dark hats. Fairytales also portray bad witches as ugly with warts on their faces and pointed noses. Yes, we know better, but labeling and prejudging is often inaccurate. We may have a fixed idea that certain people dress, speak, and act a certain way, and we don't expect a bank robber to be a tiny, gray-haired grandmotherly type--but she could.

The point is; avoid worn-out stereotyping and try to portray your characters in a fresh, original way.

Surprise me with characters that are: different, interesting and filled with unexpected qualities. That makes for a better read

Do you have a favorite cliché or one you know you shouldn't always use.

ADD it to our list.
e-mail: info@goldenquillpress.com

Writing Map 10

TRIP REVIEW

Map Directions

Style Is Your Way Of Expressing Your Ideas & Thoughts; Distinct From Other Writers

Tone Is The Overall Mood You Establish In Your Writing

Metaphors, Imagery & Simile Add Color To Your Writing

Avoid Clichés & Stereotyping

Travel Instructions — Did You?

❑ Establish Your Tone

❑ Play Metaphor, Simile, & Imagery Game & add to your

❑ Build your Bridges to Transitions & add to your

OUR GUIDES
Point You In The Right Direction

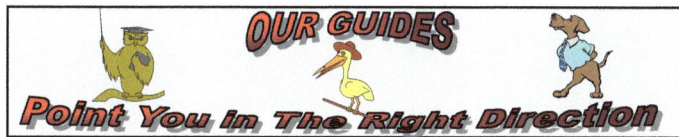

Your Writing Tone (HOOT, HOOT) sets the Mood

That makes your words sing, and CHIRP!

For a BARKING good READ!

◄ NOTE ►
Your writing style expresses your visions moving your reader to see, feel and sense not only the magic of your words, but all the meanings they convey.

Writing Map 10 — BRIDGES TO TRANSITIONS — Form

Take your characters from one place to another from one time to another and from one Chapter to another

To add a point: furthermore, in addition, finally, for example, for instance
"In addition to working for the I.S.A you will follow all Dr. Schmidt's orders, no matter what!"

Cause and Effect: because, consequently, as a result, therefore
"As a result of Brad's foolhardy scheme, he will have to face jail time."

Emphasis: above all
Above all Controller must be destroyed.

Spatial: near, far, in front of, beside, beyond, a above, below, to the right, to the left, around, inside, outside
Brad looked around, but only saw one broken vial— the spilled formula was beyond his sight.

Purpose: for this/that reason, for this/that purpose
Controller had to be destroyed or Jonathan would be a zombie forever. For that reason Brad made a deal with Cracko

To contrast: but, however, on the other hand, even though
Even though Evie knew her parents would not be happy she still went to the modeling audition

To compare: in the same way, similarly
Brad never looked at things in the same way as his parents.

Time: now, then, before, after, earlier, later, meanwhile
Jon told Brad; earlier that night he gave into temptation. He begged Sheila for more candies.

To summarize: in summary, in conclusion, to sum up
"In conclusion, Dr. Schmidt, we don't know how to destroy Controller."

_Take your characters from one place to another from one time to another and from one Chapter to another

_____
_____
_____
_____
_____
_____
_____
_____
_____
_____
_____
_____
_____
_____
_____
_____
_____
_____
_____
_____
_____
_____
_____
_____
_____
_____
_____
_____
_____

Writing Map 10   METAPHOR, IMAGERY, SIMILE   Form

METAPHOR, IMAGERY SIMILE Example:

The rain was pounding on her car's hood, but Evie didn't seem to notice. Through water drenched eyes all she could see was Rick. She'd never met anyone who knocked her off her feet the way he did. He was like a diamond in the rough; trying to hid all the facets of his personality.

As she watched him fixing her car, her heart seemed to leap out of her chest like the thunder that was blasting in the distance.

The lightening illuminated his face and once again she saw that little boy look. Everyone said he was "bad," but she could see beneath that facade to the depths of his soul. She hoped someday he'd see her that way: through the eyes of love.

Write your scene adding similes and metaphors to create vivid imagery. Use to add to your scene descriptions.

_____
_____
_____
_____
_____
_____
_____
_____
_____
_____
_____
_____
_____
_____
_____
_____
_____
_____
_____
_____
_____
_____
_____
_____
_____

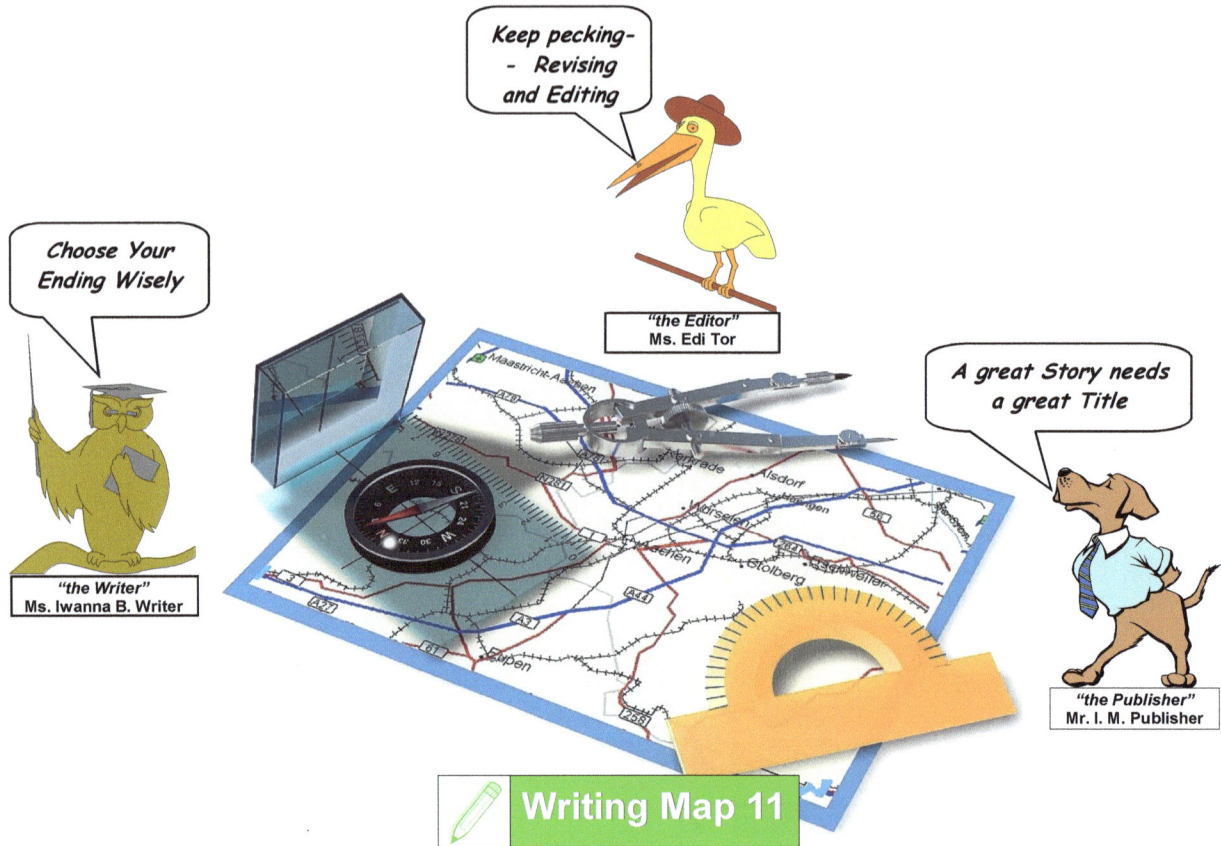

"the Editor"
Ms. Edi Tor

Keep pecking-- Revising and Editing

Choose Your Ending Wisely

"the Writer"
Ms. Iwanna B. Writer

A great Story needs a great Title

"the Publisher"
Mr. I. M. Publisher

Writing Map 11

FINISHING WITH A FLAIR

Now that your story has all the elements that best sellers are made of, you want to be sure you give the same attention to the ending. Many times when a writer gets to the this point, they rush to get finished. Taking time to plot out the ending will prove worthwhile; a great ending will leave your readers panting for more. One of the key elements to a great ending is for the story to come full circle. Full circle means: you have tied up all the loose ends, revealed all the details that you withheld along the way, and as your readers turn to the last page you leave them wishing for more.

Poorly written endings can turn good books into a, "I'm sorry I read it" book!

Don't let the reader catch the worm-- that loose end you forgot to tie up

If there's no barking ending – there's no future for the author

Just like hooking your readers in the beginning and keeping them interested all the way through; the ending is pivotal. There are many possibilities for ways to create a great ending and here are just a few: Surprise, Poetic, Summary.

Many Roads lead to a Successful Ending

As with the rest of your story, your style and story line has been a determining factor and your ending is no different. How you end your book should follow the same pattern as how you have written the book—but this is the time when you can get very creative. Your beginning hook got your reader to continue reading-- now take advantage of the chance to WOW your reader one last time! It's important. Endings do not have to be long and drawn out—but they must be fantastic.

Surprise Ending: You've been leading the reader along and the reader expects a certain ending—but you change direction and pull off the unexpected.

Poetic Ending: All's well that ends well. This is a popular way to end a book—and it generally satisfies the reader. Many readers want books to end on a "happy note."

Summation Ending: The story summation, usually by a main character reiterating the events that led to that point.

There's also another ending that sets your book up for a sequel called a

Continuation Ending. This type of ending leaves the reader with a new situation, or a question that's still hanging when the book ends —usually to be resolved in the next book.

Alert— Alert: Our Wise Guides Note:

Some endings may even have a little of all the formulas, but the best endings are not drawn out but if you've written a book 300 pages in length; summing up the whole book in a page or two, seems a bit abrupt. Don't let your readers down at the end— nothing is worse for a reader than to have spent time with your entire story only to be rushed or let down and   disappointed at the end.

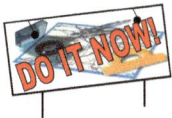

Get your Writing Map 11 **END DETAILING** Form
from your Travel Kit at the back of this chapter

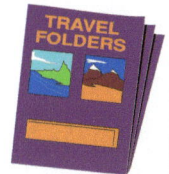

Decide on your ending style and write your ending. You may want to try out a few possibilities before you decide on the final one.

Finally! You've finished a First Draft — Celebrate!!! Next, sit down and CONGRATULATE yourself. This is a BIG STEP. As soon as you've enjoyed the moment, shared it with family and friends — reveled in your success, and had a good nights sleep, then we can continue on the last leg of the journey.

Onto the Next Road.

TITLE: Let's go back to your original title. Many times when we finish a story the original title may still be fantastic -- but it may also be very wrong. You'll need to be even more objective at this time.

A Word About Titles

The title of your book is important because it's what your reader sees first. Many readers judge a book by its title and decide whether they want to take the book off the shelf. Now that you know this element can be your first chance to make a good impression, choose your title carefully.

Think of your favorite book — movie, TV show – then change the Title – If the only information you had was a Title — would you still choose it. That's how important a Title can be!

Play the Title Game: When we change the following Titles, see how it affects you.

Gone With the Wind	to	A Plantation in the South
Carrie	to	Strange Girl at the Prom
Star Trek	to	Journey through the Solar Systems
The Wizard of Oz	to	Dreams of Far Away Places

Which would you choose?

The same analysis is needed with your Title. Here are a few tips to keep in mind. The title could tell what the book is about in an eye-catching way. But remember Titles shouldn't divulge Too Much! Some Titles promise adventure while others a hint of romance, but Titles can entice readers in such a way that they can't wait to read that book.

Study book titles to see how they tie in with the contents and message of a book. Look at the book cover. What does it convey? Study both front and back covers to see how the written material and cover design tie in with the title. Sometimes a title like, "Gone with the Wind," or our book, "Code 47 to BREV Force," doesn't mean anything to a reader. However, the title takes on meaning and when combined with the cover design conveys the message of the book.

Note how some books have a subtitle: Sometimes when a title is unclear, a subtitle is used. Sub-titles can also be further inducement to the reader:

"The Legend of Black Sandy Beach - Survival on a Deserted Island
"Rags To Riches -- The Stock Market Killing
"TELL IT TO THE FUTURE-- Have I Got A Story For You…"

Some questions to ask about your title: Does your book have a direct promise? "Helpful Hints to Lose Weight Fast" Note: Be Sure Your Book Doesn't Promise Something It Doesn't Deliver!

Does the title identify with your story? "Justice is Blind" If your story has nothing to do with fairness, a trial or something in that category – it may be a great Title, but not for your book.

Our Wise Guides Suggest:

If you' re looking to sell your story and the Editor and Publisher suggest a Title change — remember they have experience with books that sell — and one's that don't!

Get your Writing Map 11 **TITLE DETAILING** Form
from your Travel Kit at the back of this chapter

First skim through your first draft and try to identify what elements would make the title fit your story. Jot them down. Write your original Title and see if the elements of your story lead to that Title or if a better Title surfaces. You can also ask family and friends, especially those who read.

EDITING-REVISING

The Road to the Final Manuscript

Now that you've completed your first draft, we can get back on the highway that will lead to your final manuscript. This may seem like a long and windy road, and you may be asking yourself why you need to take that road — the answer is simple — all your hard work got your ideas down on paper. Now your story needs to be perfected. You need to take on this part of your journey with the same planning and enthusiasm as the previous parts of your trip. If you do, you'll find this last leg of the journey to be very exciting…and thrilling as you realize how close you are to the finished story.

During this part of your journey Mrs. Edi Tor and Mr. I. M. Publisher, will be your navigators. In order to properly edit and revise your draft you'll need to be very objective, and leave your ego at the door. You may feel every word you've written, is a gem; every thought incredible and every sentence and character necessary -- but "it ain't necessarily so!" If you want to make your journey effective, you need to stop and carefully analyze what you've written.

If you can't do that, don't beat yourself up — everyone needs a travel agent at some time. That is why there are professional editors.

For our purposes let's assume you are raring to go and have pointed your vehicle in the right direction -- here's your road map through this hilly terrain. Answer these questions as you begin to read your first draft aloud. Try to listen as the passenger, rather than the driver. This reading is not for grammar and spelling mistakes, it's a   rethinking of all aspects of your story.

Take out your Travel Folder and refer back to ALL your Writing Plan Detailing Forms. As you read your first draft, look back to be sure you've used all the important information and that you   didn't mix up character details. Decide what improvements you can make to turn your first draft into your edited manuscript.

DRAFT TO MANUSCRIPT
CHECK LIST:

☐ <u>Does your story have an interesting beginning?</u>
  - ☐ Are the first 10 pages slow or fast paced
  - ☐ Does the story get started in those first 10 pages
  - ☐ What has been introduced to make the reader want to turn to the next page
  - ☐ Is there an easily recognizable lead or a hook that will hold your reader's interest
  - ☐ Is the hook unique (not usual or expected)
  - ☐ Is the hook strong enough to keep the reader turning pages
  - ☐ Does the hook appear in the first few pages

☐ <u>Are your characters dynamic?</u>
  - ☐ Do they cause the reader to root for them or hate them
  - ☐ Are they realistic
  - ☐ Do they each have a goal or reason for being in the story
  - ☐ Does the dialogue move the story along
  - ☐ Do your characters express what is happening by dialogue, as well as by their actions
  - ☐ Do the character descriptions bring to mind a visual picture

☐ <u>Is the time and place clear and interesting?</u>
  - ☐ Is the main setting memorable
  - ☐ Does the place and time fit with your story and work well for the story

☐ <u>Has the story line included problems that need to be solved?</u>
  - ☐ Were the problems clearly explained so the reader could follow the flow
  - ☐ Before the end of the story were all the problems and conflicts resolved

☐ <u>Were all the loose ends tied up so the reader will be satisfied?</u>
  - ☐ Has every characters situation been explained and wrapped up by the end of the story

Now really step back – and think about the questions Our Wise Guides are asking

Writing Map 11

TRIP REVIEW

Map Directions

Title Is The Judge That Gets Your Book Off The Shelf

Endings Are As Important As Beginnings

Celebrate Finishing The First Draft

Revise and Edit As If You Were Reading The Book For The First Time

Travel Instructions — Did You?

❑ Devise a Great Ending and add to your

❑ Play the Title Game and add to your

❑ Use your Detailing Forms to help you Revise and Edit

OUR GUIDES

Point You in The Right Direction

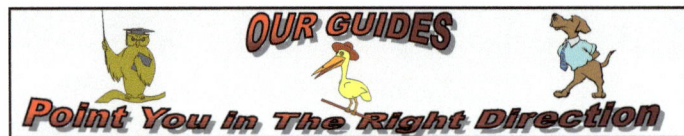

"A Wise Old, Young Owl"
What a GREAT Title

Keep revising and
editing until your
story sings

A Great Ending gets
my tail wagging

◄ NOTE ►

Remember the reader can't get into your head – and, you can't always assume
what a reader knows – or understands --

Writing Map 11   ENDING DETAILING   Form

Summation Ending

The BREV Force hung up their costumes after the press conference and returned to their normal lives. Brian enrolled in Norton University and Ginger helped him get into the routine of college life. He also got a job as a computer specialist with the management company at Compustock Mall. Brian still thought about Robin, but never mentioned her to anyone.

Brad was trying to balance school, work and Francoise who was the only girl he was dating.

Evie was happier than ever. Her job as a fashion designer apprentice got her a first chance to design a new wedding collection, under her name, *"designs by eve-lyn!"*

Martin and Vivian returned to their research work for National Security and enjoyed new baby, Marcella.

Remy now headed up the International Alliance of Scientists and was seated in his new office at their headquarters in Geneva. He was beginning to get acclimated to his new position and into a routine of commuting back and forth, by teleportation to his new home in Island Falls.

Having arrived early that morning, Remy waited while his holographic secretary reported the day's schedule and began processing the daily reports which were coming in from all over the world..

While the Rhapsody played on the Symphonic speaker System, in the background Remy relaxed with his morning coffee before getting to the work at hand. He had missed seeing his daughter Francoise that morning before he left and was eagerly awaiting a "good morning" e-mail. He clicked on his inbox in hopes of finding her friendly smile.

< "47 K incoming.">

He wondered what she was sending. He moved the mouse to open the file and sat staring at the message:

<*"U R the 1!"*>

The End

(NOTE: This finally paragraph can also make the ending a Surprise and/or a Continuation)

Your Ending Choice: _____

_____
_____
_____
_____
_____
_____
_____
_____
_____
_____
_____
_____
_____
_____
_____
_____
_____
_____
_____
_____
_____
_____
_____
_____
_____
_____
_____
_____
_____
_____
_____
_____
_____
_____

Writing Map 11   TITLE DETAILING   Form

Original title: Teen Force

Elements:

Teenager become superheroes Force against computer virus

Respond to Code to become super heroes

Names equals combination of their names

B = Br ad and Br ian

R = r and Remy

E = Ev ie

V = v and Vivian

47 =is numeric value of names

Possible Titles:

Teens against Computer Virus

Becoming Super Heroes

Words that might form a title —

Teen , Super, heroes, Force, computer, virus, Code, Names, BREV, 47

Possible New Title

Code 47 to BREV Force

Compare to your original

Teen Force

Which do you believe is a better title?

Code 47 to BREV Force

(when you go through your draft for editing and revising -- keep this Title in mind, but be open to the possibility of another Title jumping out at you).

Writing Map 12

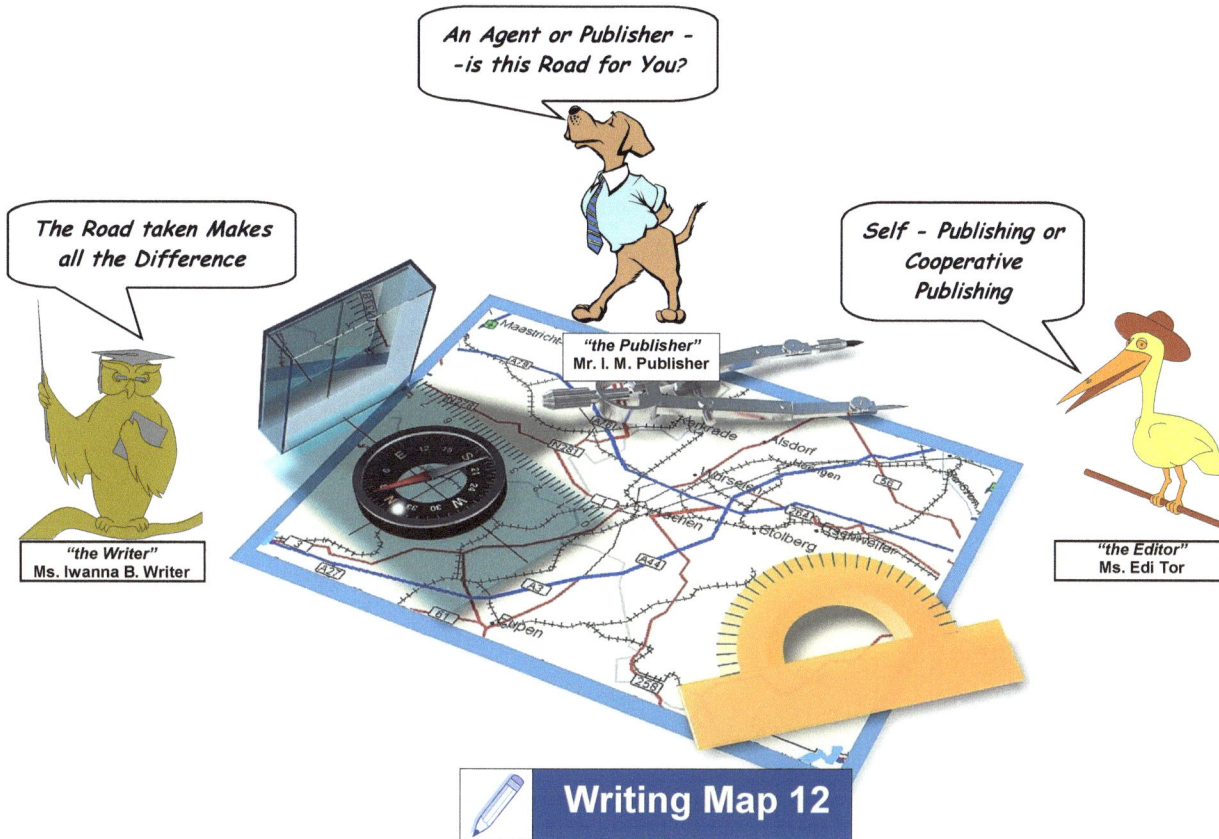

TAKE YOUR STORY TO MARKET

Now that we have a finished manuscript we're almost at the end of our journey. You've traveled many roads to get here and now you need to make the most of your progress. With so many possibilities we need to first decide the right direction to take. But before we can do that we need to dress the part.

Manuscript Preparation Checklist

This is similar to the draft checklist, but now we're adding the finishing touches. When preparing your manuscript, stick to the basics. The Sample Forms on the next few pages will help you understand proper format. On the Cover Page in the right hand corner you need to indicate the word count. If you work with a computer go to: Tools, then click on word count. This box will come up:>>>

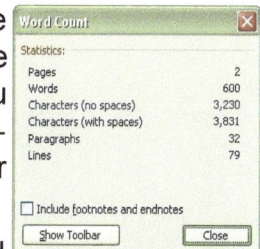

If you don't have a computer, you'll need to use the old fashioned method - COUNT! Estimate by counting average number of words across the page, multiplied by average number of lines down. Example: 10 words across x 25 lines = 250 words per page. Multiply this by the number of pages in your finished work to obtain an approximate number of words. Approximate is usually close enough, but the computer will give you an exact number. **Note: When revising your work—cutting or adding copy—always re-check your word count.**

COVER PAGE ← FIRST Page **BEFORE** Your Manuscript

- 1" -

Your Name
Street Address
City, State, Zip Code ← Your Personal Information
Phone Number
Email Address

* Word Count

Total Number Of Words In Manuscript

FONT USE ONLY
12 Point Arial or
Times Roman Type

- 1" -

TITLE ← **ALL CAPS**

By ← **Beginning Cap Then Lower Case**

Your Name

Center Title & By Line

SPECIAL NOTES:

Use 8 1/2" x 11" plain white, good quality paper. Type on only

one side of the paper.

Generally, you will have about 250 to 300 words per page.

- 1" -

CHAPTER BEGINNING PAGE

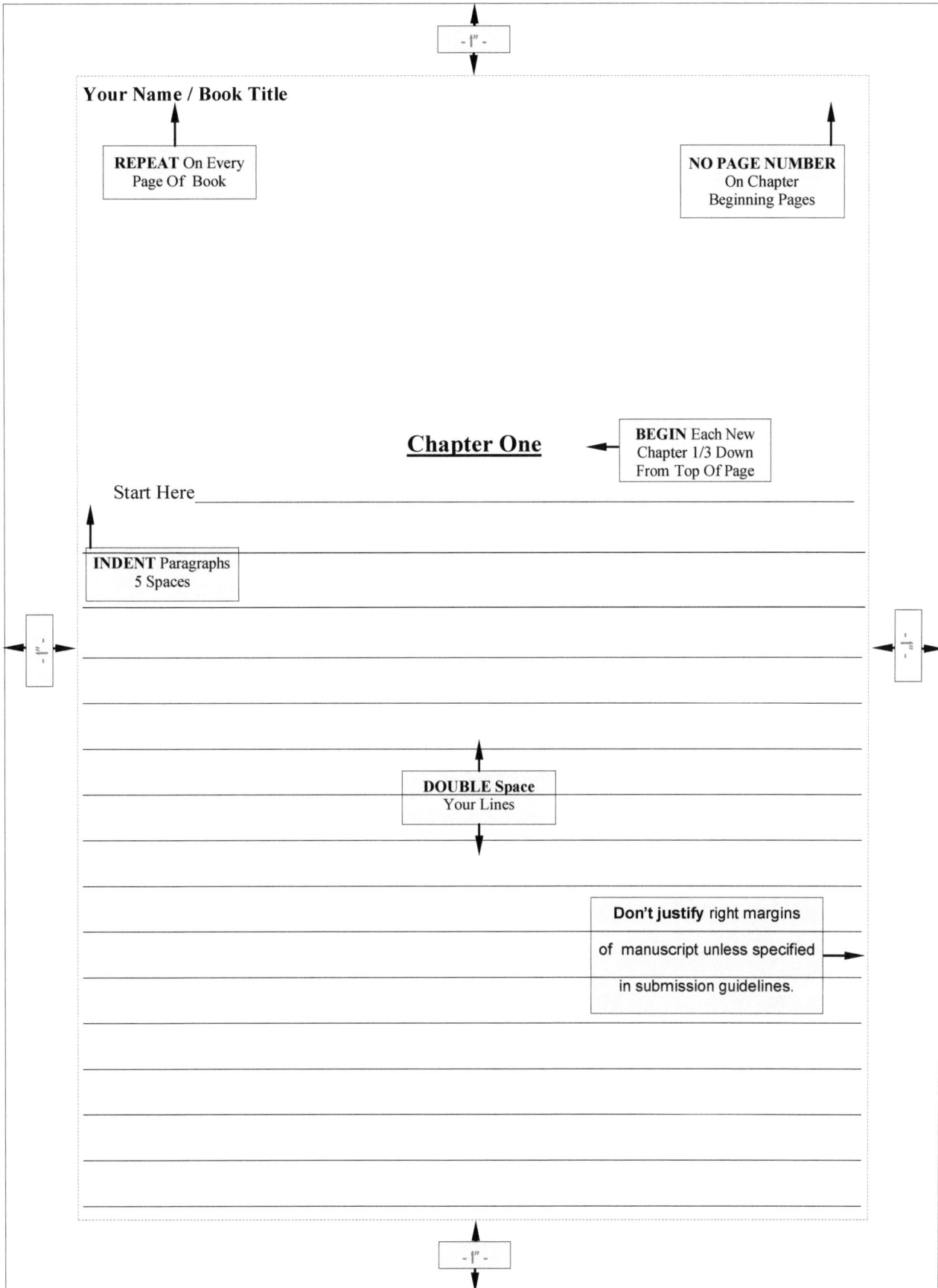

- 1" -

Your Name / Book Title

REPEAT On Every
Page Of Book

NO PAGE NUMBER
On Chapter
Beginning Pages

Chapter One

BEGIN Each New
Chapter 1/3 Down
From Top Of Page

Start Here

INDENT Paragraphs
5 Spaces

- 1" -

- 1" -

DOUBLE Space
Your Lines

Don't justify right margins
of manuscript unless specified
in submission guidelines.

- 1" -

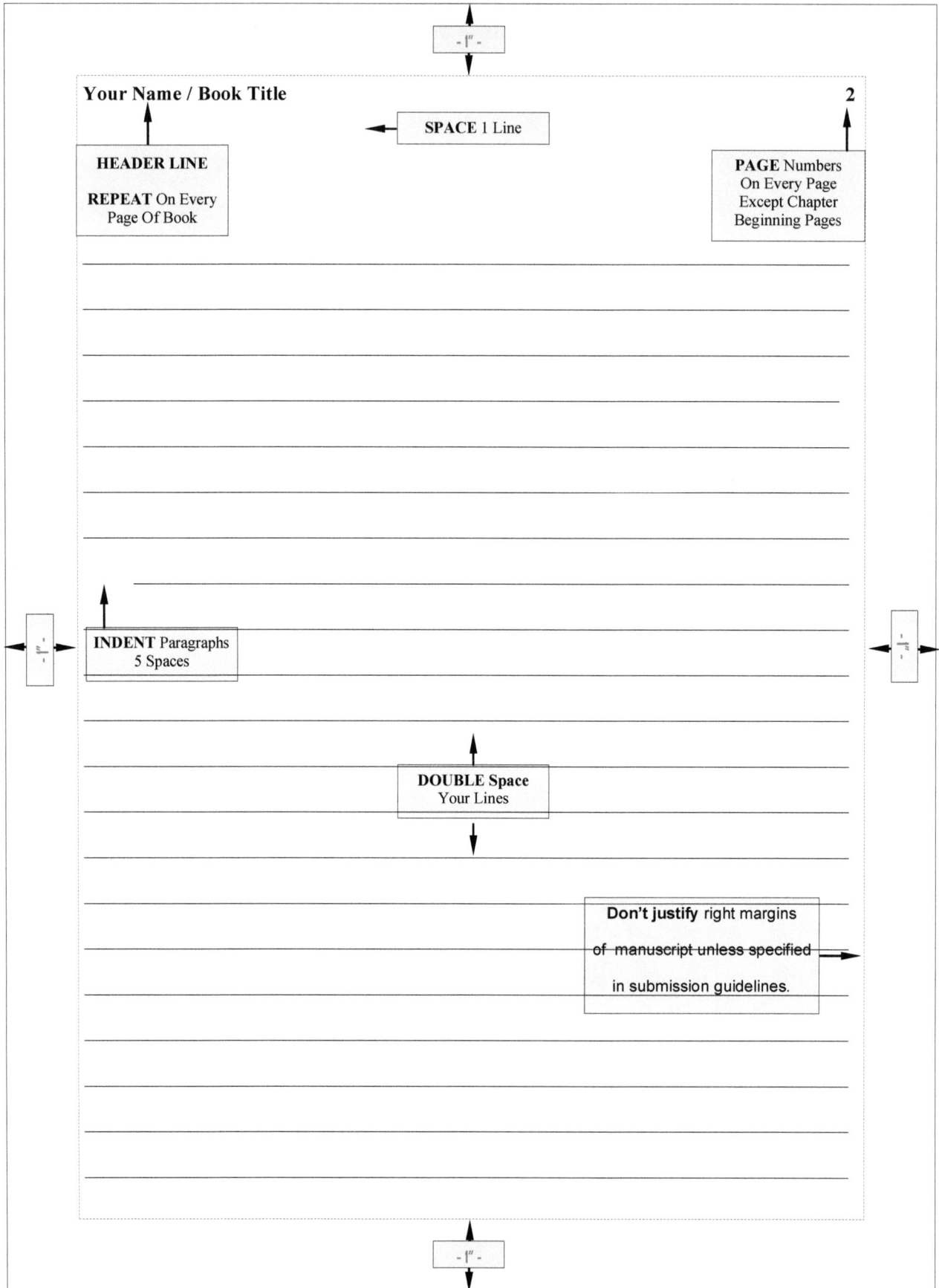

TYPICAL PAGE

- 1" -

Your Name / Book Title 2

SPACE 1 Line

HEADER LINE

REPEAT On Every
Page Of Book

PAGE Numbers
On Every Page
Except Chapter
Beginning Pages

- 1" -

INDENT Paragraphs
5 Spaces

- 1" -

DOUBLE Space
Your Lines

Don't justify right margins
of manuscript unless specified
in submission guidelines.

- 1" -

Just Along for the Ride

If you've written your story just for yourself, your family and friends or to leave for future generations, then this is the end of your road. You Did IT! You now have a FINISHED MANUSCRIPT, – and We Are VERY PROUD of YOU! Even if your work was just for yourself, we suggest you consider making copies and giving them to those who'll appreciate your efforts and enjoy the fruits of your labors.

We also hope since you've worked so hard, you might now consider publishing, as an option. Even if you have no intention of selling to bookstores, you may want your story converted into a conventional book. If this journey has given you the slightest urge, please, get back on the road with us and continue the journey to that end.

Admiring the Scenery on Genré Highway

Establishing your Genré means to decide on the category (Genré) for your writing: If you're not sure what category is right, visit your local library or bookstore and check other books in the genré you believe is similar to yours. By a process of elimination you should be able to correctly identify your genré. — Here's a list of some choices:

Action	Horror
Adventure	Mainstream
Biographical	Mystery
Children	Romance
Contemporary	Science-Fiction
Crime	Suspense
Fantasy	Western
Historical	Young Adult

While browsing amongst the books, note that non-fiction covers a wide selection of categories. How to books, Cook books, and Business related books are just a few.

Now that we know which genré your story fits into, next we need to see whose publishing what you're writing. There are many good tools on the market to help you familiarize yourself with the publishing industry. Writer's Market and Literary Marketplace are two sources for searching out what publisher's are looking for and their requirements. Just keep in mind, these reference sources are published annually and information may be out of date. Publishers Weekly is another important resource which can be found at most libraries. It's chock full of who's publishing what, trends, reviews and additional information.

Publisher's web sites have also become very informative. Many publisher's have internet sites that include: books they've published, their imprints, and some even include submission requirements and e-mail addresses for editors.

It's also acceptable to call publishing houses and request guidelines, or verify editor's names and positions. Another way to get the information is to scan the shelves of libraries and bookstores to find books similar to yours. Check out who published them. Many times just by flipping through the front and back you may find an acknowledgement or thank you with the editor's name.

Driving to your Genré

The book business is genré driven so first be sure the publisher you have chosen to send your work to publishes in your genré. Suppose your novel is science fiction and you find this listing:

Silver Lane an imprint (division) of Meredith House.
Silver Lane--Currently publishing 9 books a year;
6 Science Fiction and 3 Historical Non-Fiction.
First time novelists accepted. Bob Bara; Editor-in-Chief, Mary Meed; Science Fiction Editor, George Gee; Historical Editor.
We respond within 3 months. (555-555-5555)
330 Next St., New Book, VA 00000

Major Publishers usually have many imprints — be sure you contact the one that's right for your book

the Editor- in- Chief is rarely the first to read a new manuscript, and a senior editor is always better to approach then a junior

You should send to the science fiction (genré) editor, Mary Meed. If the listing doesn't indicate what to send, you should call and ask for guidelines, or look them up on the web.

Alert, Alert: Our Experts Agree:

NEVER SEND

your manuscript to a publisher whose listing states,
"we do not accept unsolicited manuscripts"

This phrase, "Unsolicited manuscripts," is common in the publishing industry. Basically it means, don't call us, we'll call you!

Another phrase to be aware of is: **"DO NOT ACCEPT MULTIPLE SUBMISSIONS"**

OUR GUIDES ADVISE:

If this phrase is in the guidelines it means the publisher will not look at your work if you are sending it to another publisher simultaneously. So decide which publisher you believe you have the best chance with and only send the requested materials to that publisher. If you receive a rejection, or no response from that publisher, then you are free to send to any others.

Remember also, if a listing states, "agented submissions only" you can only submit through an agent.

All Dressed Up with Somewhere to Go -- Manuscript Submission

Now that you know your genré and which publisher might be interested in your type of work, you're ready to begin the task of marketing. We've met many writers who don't have a clue about this part of the process: marketing their work. They don't read all the guidelines, or ignore them, thinking, "my book is just what that editor is looking for." Or, they just send out manuscripts to publishers at random, only to have their hopes dashed by rejection after rejection. Also, because they don't understand the publishers requirements, they send the full manuscript, instead of what the publisher asked for. Some writers don't include a SASE (self-addressed stamped envelope, or manuscript box) and don't receive their manuscript back—only a letter). This is VERY COSTLY and a BIG WASTE OF TIME!

Always send Publishers ONLY what they request

Our Experts Agree:

DON"T SEND YOUR MANUSCRIPT
unless it says to do so in the submission guidelines.

When you do send your work, be sure to include a cover letter with your return address and phone number. Also include materials and adequate postage for the manuscript's return to you. Many first time writers make the mistake of only sending their manuscripts to the most successful larger publishers and ignore the smaller houses. Our Experts suggest you may find it easier to market to a small house, but you should still research both small and large publishing firms.

Editors don't have time to pass work around, so don't send your travel article to the food editor!

Other Avenues to Market First

If you want to get your name out there before you approach agents or publishers, try essays and short stories for magazines and local newspapers. Study the contents of a variety of publications and look for trends. Generally, magazine editors need stories and articles months in advance and will expect you to follow specific guidelines.

The masthead in magazines will list the editors and their titles.

Helen Hill - Food Editor
Steven Chase - Education
Myra Morton - Garden Editor
Peter Thomas - Travel

In order to correctly market a short story or article you must obtain guidelines and be sure the finished work is sent to the proper editor.

Take the Right Manuscript Submission Exit

Before sending anything, ascertain exactly what the publisher wants. Many publishers require a query* or synopsis* before seeing the entire manuscript. (*see more information on next page). Sometimes they may also want to see the first three chapters. Different publishers have different submission requirements so to save time; find out first!

Even a great story idea can be rejected if it is poorly written

Drive one block and turn on Query Street

When you're ready to turn in the direction of publishers and agents, you may need to write a query. To query means to "ask", and in this case you're asking a publisher to consider your work. You hope their interest will be piqued enough by your fantastic query to want to see more. This letter of inquiry requires your best thinking and writing. This is your opportunity to sell yourself and your book.

The query letter should be written as a sales pitch, or a movie trailer; summing up your book in no more than one exciting page. Generally you don't need a separate cover letter. Be sure you include all the best elements of your story — hero, villains, conflict, resolution and leave the editor with a teaser. Most importantly show the editor your style of writing. Don't forget to check spelling and grammar check.

Write that Exciting Query that reads like the best introduction or back cover for your book:

Points to Include:

- ❏ Opening sentence or paragraph "Hook"
- ❏ Fantastic story Premise
- ❏ A quote or paragraph that really sells your idea
- ❏ Identify your target reader
- ❏ What makes this story similar to other best selling novels, or different enough to be a crowd pleaser
- ❏ Always include something about yourself and mention previous writing that shows your ability. (note: if you're a first time novelist and don't have any other writing credit, tell why you're qualified to write this book)
- ❏ Be sure to thank the editor for his or her time
- ❏ Include a SASE (self addressed stamped envelope)

Be sure you have the right editor's name and that it's spelled correctly.

Don't send a completed manuscript unless the editor asks for it. Also check the guidelines to see whether the editor wants you to send any chapters or other materials along with the query.

An editor and publisher were once heard to say:

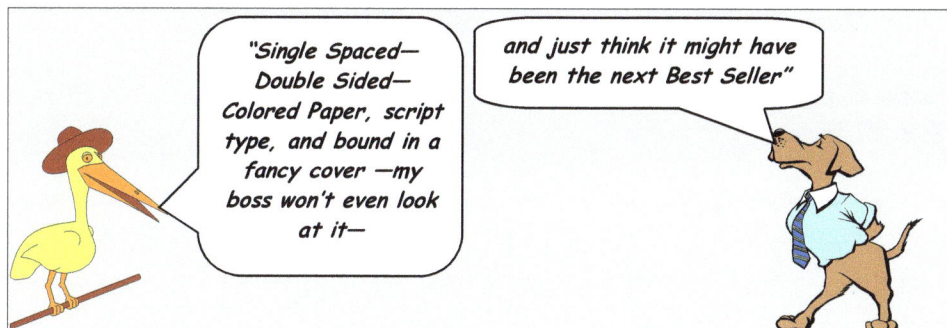

So keep it simple and properly prepared and you'll get started on the right road.

Note:

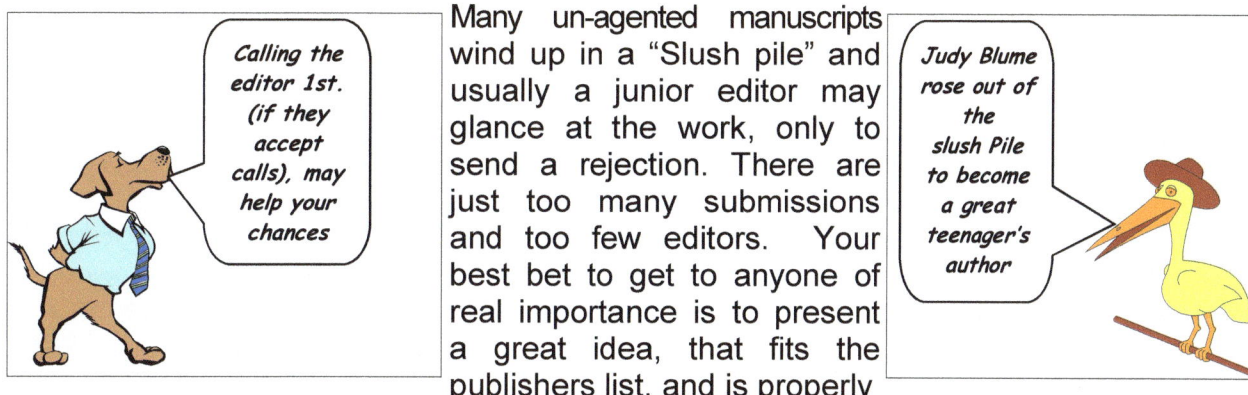

Many un-agented manuscripts wind up in a "Slush pile" and usually a junior editor may glance at the work, only to send a rejection. There are just too many submissions and too few editors. Your best bet to get to anyone of real importance is to present a great idea, that fits the publishers list, and is properly prepared to wow the editor and publisher. It does happen!

Should You E-mail Queries?

It's best to find out if e-mail is accepted. If so, go for it. If not, go the usual postal letter route.

If you would like professional assistance in preparing, or editing your query you can visit our website at: www.thewritesource.homestead.com/services.html

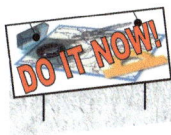

Get your Writing Map 12 **TRACKING DETAIL** Form from your Travel Kit at the back of this chapter **When Completed store in your Travel Folder** you can make extra copies or download the forms at http://www.goldenquillpress.homestead.com/ideaforms.html

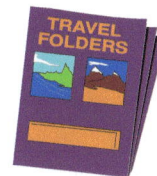

PS This Form can also be used for Synopsis, Proposals and Manuscripts.

SEE SAMPLE QUERY LETTER ON NEXT PAGE

SAMPLE QUERY LETTER

Write a Query for Your Book. Here's an sample to follow:

15 Willow Sweep Rd
Scotts land, BB 22222

July 15, 2009

Children's Editions
34 Bookland Ave. 16th Floor
New Market, NN 001111
Attention: Marian Rusen, Sr. Editor

Dear Ms. Rusen:

"The Adventures of the We Clan" brilliantly unfolds for children 5-8 years of age, as they experience what it's like to be different and what standing up for themselves means. The We Clan gives us a portrayal of characters that will delight children with their uniqueness. The Clan will also help children have a better understanding of relationships, being different in our world, its animals and other species.

This adventure/fantasy takes children into the imaginary world of these "Smurf" size people who live in a cave. They have strong moral views and family values that are nurtured in a very structured society. Problems occur when a normal size man, who seems like a giant to them, enters their cave and steals a treasured harp they use in all their celebrations. Horrendous unhappiness befalls the We Clan who now must challenge the "Giant" for their possession. The reader experiences many adventures on their escapade to retrieve the harp and enjoys a touching moment as they are befriended by neighboring animals. With the help of these new found friends, they storm the Giant's Castle; find the harp and barely escape the Giant's fury. They emerge victorious and return home with the animals to celebrate

To test market this idea I went to a local school and the response was overwhelming. Not only did the story keep and hold the children's attention, they were so excited they couldn't wait to hear how the story would end. They voted for their favorite characters, booed the Giant and picked their favorite cover.
Strong characters, imaginative experiences and life lessons give this story the type of possibilities for success that your company has achieved with the H. Possem Series. I am sure you will love the We Clan and clamor to see more . The first three chapters of the manuscript are enclosed as per your submission guidelines and a SASE for return of materials. Thank you for your time and consideration.

Sincerely,

Barbara Bee

Synopsis Road

Sometimes an editor will want a synopsis. This is a complete outline of your book. They may want it chapter by chapter or just the major events. Length also can vary from one or two pages to 10 plus; double-spaced. But the most important thing for you to know is a synopsis needs to read like a story outline and yet be as interesting and exciting as the book itself. It must show your writing style. The synopsis is always written: in present tense, third person and should weave your story from one sentence to the next. Tell all the points: don't hint at or imply and be sure to include: the Hook, beginning middle, climax and end. Keep dialogue to the barest minimum, if at all. A good synopsis should be able to sell you and your story, so don't forget to check for grammar and spelling errors.

If you would like professional assistance in preparing, or editing your synopsis visit our website at: www.info@goldenquillpress.com

Detailing the Road of Proposals:

Proposals are in-depth analysis of your book. They are generally required for non-fiction. A Proposal should include: marketing and sales projections, competitive works, author's information and promotional skills, table of contents, chapter by chapter outline, sample chapters and synopsis. Proposals are very detailed. We recommend getting complete guidelines and looking at sample proposals before even attempting this task.

If you would like professional assistance in preparing, or editing your proposal you can check our website at: www.info@goldenquillpress.com

Sending your work to Publishers

A word about sending you work to publishers. Many times we've heard first time novelists concern about someone stealing story ideas. Usually publishers have heard every type of idea concept at one time or another and most stories are just different versions of a similar theme. Of course it could happen, so we can not give you a guarantee. All we can say is, if you're really concerned, mail a copy of your manuscript to yourself and do not open it. The United States Postal date stamp proves the date you sent the finished work to yourself. That may at least give you some peace of mind. We are also asked about copyright. Most first time authors feel they must have their work copy written. This is also not necessary. Under U.S. copyright laws the author is the owner of all rights to their literary work. When your book is published official copyright will be obtained for you as the author.

Major Publishers usually have many imprints — be sure you contact the one that's right for your book

Alert – Alert Our Experts Suggest keep your first drafts as proof of your original idea.

Telephoning Editors

When your query is being considered be aware of the timeline given and don't telephone before a reasonable amount of time. If the guidelines indicate 3 months, wait the full amount of time and add two weeks before calling.

The Billboard Says, "The Editor wants to read YOUR entire Manuscript"

An editor's job is to obtain the most marketable materials possible, so if they want to see your manuscript you're on the right road. Be sure you send a properly prepared manuscript,(see our guidelines earlier in this chapter). Remember no rubber bands, paper clips — fancy folders, just loose in a manuscript box. (These can be gotten at stationary or office supply stores). Some writers want to send a picture of what their cover should look like, the back cover and a list of thank you's etc. Again we remind you, do not send anything but the manuscript, and be sure to enclose a SASE (self addressed stamped envelope, or box with enough postage) if you want your work returned. Always enclose a cover letter reminding the editor you were asked to send the manuscript

When you start to send out queries and manuscripts keep a log of dates and editor's names. This will help you track the manuscript dates sent, returned and the results. This form will also help you know which editors not to resend. Sometimes editors may change or there may be two editors in the same division — so keep your records accurate. Also, keep any notes or letters of rejection. Be sure to check publisher's listings often. Many times publishers might be looking for exactly what you have 6 months down the line, or editors change and the new one may be interested in your work.

Hard Copy or Disk

When an editor wants to see your entire manuscript and requests both hard copy (on paper) and disk, (computer disk) be sure you use a program that is compatible with what they're requesting. Inquire if you are not sure.

Understanding the Agent's Role

If you decide the direct road to the publisher is blocked or closed to you, an agent may be another answer. Getting an agent can be as difficult as finding a publisher. Use the same resources to get a list of agent's names. Then do your research and check each agent's background to be sure that agent works with your genré and has sold work to publishers. Do this before contacting them. There are many fine agents, but unfortunately, there are some so called "agents" who are just looking for a way to make money off a desperate writer and may not be legitimate. Remember to be an agent, all you have to do is say, "I'm an agent!" Also, if an agent asks for money be on the alert. There are associations and guilds that can advise you if this is a fair practice. Just do your homework and you'll be fine!

The good agent works for you. They work with you to get the best deal for your book. An agent finds the right publisher and then negotiates the contract and legal aspects regarding your work.

When you're looking for an agent, keep in mind that many may not accept your type of writing or take on first time authors

If you take the Wrong Turn and your Work is Rejected?

Authors in our workshops have told us they could paper walls with the rejection letters they've received, before getting that all-important "yes." They've also confirmed our belief that if you have a great story, that is well written; you'll eventually find the right match: the right publisher.

Getting a rejection note or letter should not be taken personally. The editor or agent may not accept your book for many reasons other than it wasn't good: another book on the same topic may be in the works, the publisher can't take anything else on, or the budget is too tight. Another point to be aware of is that the publishing house may only publish a specific number of certain types of books during their budget year. They may like your book, but have no money for its purchase, or have reached their quota for that type of book.

Be happy if an editor or agent takes time to give you a few words of encouragement. You may be advised to try another publisher. Do it! Do it over and over, and keep learning with each submission. Authors try for years to get published. Many famous authors experienced numerous rejections including the now famous author of Harry Potter, J. K. Rowling, and the best selling author Stephen King. They kept banging on doors until they got their first break — so you'll be in good company. Like them, you must believe in your story: your dream. Never give up until you've exhausted every avenue Keep your rejection letters; not to paper a wall, but to remind you to be persistent, and remember how many famous authors were once just like you; first-time novelist.

Even a great story idea can be rejected if it is poorly written

Another Highway To Consider

Sometimes it's hard to be objective about your work. Friends and family want to cheer you on but may not be the best critic. You may want to seek professional advice. Published authors, editors and publishers can guide you regarding your work. You might want to get a professional opinion or an evaluation. You can do this before you begin sending to publishers or after you've received rejections

For more information about evaluations or consultations visit our website at: www.info@goldenquillpress.com

When Your Work Is Accepted

Don't give up movie and TV rights that might be worth more $$$ than you'll make on the book

Of course if your story isn't suited for movies or TV , then get the best book deal possible

When your work is accepted, if you don't have an agent, it may be advisable to seek legal counsel. Even though most contracts are standard — you may be able to negotiate for rights you didn't even know you have. You should always read any legal papers carefully before signing and ask questions when something isn't clear. Advances and royalty percentages will be negotiated and then a final contract will be drawn up listing your rights and the rights you have given to the publisher. If there're rights you want to keep, you need be sure you haven't negotiated those rights away, and have a full understanding of what is stated in the final contract.

Our Experts Agree: A Literary Attorney Should Be Consulted When Your Work is Accepted By a Publisher

Once you begin to work with a publisher you may be assigned an editor, and you may be asked to rewrite, make changes, delete or add copy. The editor's job is to guide you to make your work more marketable. Editors are always pleased when a manuscript is so well written that it needs little or no revisions. The copy editor will check your grammar, punctuation, spelling and more. A smart author will make the copy editor's job easy by doing a line by line editing before submitting the manuscript. You may also be required to submit all your editing changes by a certain date. Your contract may detail dates for revisions and if you don't comply, your publisher may have the right to ask for the return of any advance paid to you, or hold up other money. Therefore, it's extremely important that you adhere to those dates. Also be aware that if you want something changed, it must be approved before that final date. Publishers invest a great deal of money, time and personnel in your work and have a set budget with projected dates for galley's, reviews and marketing. Pre-publication and actual publication dates and tours are set up in advance. Any delays can change the whole time-table and be very costly.

Many book deals have penalties if work is not delivered on time.

Getting on the Road to Publishing

When your work is accepted, you should set up a bookkeeping system to record income from any advance and royalties. All your expenses related to writing and publishing your book should be kept and recorded for tax purposes.

Our Experts Agree: A tax specialist should be consulted to help you understand the process and advise you regarding your taxes.

Your Star Walk of Fame

Publishers expect you to do your part to help sell your book. Most publishers want to know you better so they can properly promote your book. Some questions you may be asked are:

☐ Are you willing to do book signings and tour?

☐ Do you have public speaking experience?

☐ Would you be able to address audiences at organizations, schools, colleges, and businesses?

☐ Would you be able to handle interviews with magazines, newspapers, television or radio?

☐ Do you know your competitors?

☐ Have you looked at the features and benefits of your book as compared to others?

☐ Why is your book better?

To sum it up, you're expected to look, act, and speak the part of the successful author when in the public eye. This doesn't mean all authors travel, appear on TV or have to address live audiences. The nature of your work helps the publisher determine how to promote and publicize your book. The point is, the more you can offer the publisher in promoting your work; the better.

Other Avenues of Publication:

Self-Publishing

A number of best-selling books by famous authors have been self-published. Some of these have later been picked up by major publishers or have become motion pictures. If you want to keep full control of your work and have the time, energy, money, and contacts, you might prefer self-publishing where all the decisions are yours.

Self-publishing has advantages and disadvantages to consider and is not necessarily for everyone. You need to be aware that unless you have contacts and marketing know-how, your sales may be limited. Not being familiar with publishing: your costs may be higher, you may order more books than you need, or are able to sell. You have to wear many hats: author, publisher, marketer, promoter, shipper, etc. You may not be able to devote the time and needed resources to make your book a success. Again, it's good business to get all the information you can from more than one source before considering self-publishing. Read a few books on the subject, talk to others who have self-published, and be ready to invest a little more than pocket money.

Cooperative Publishing

Another alternative to self-publishing is Cooperative Publishing. When you want to self-publish, but don't know how and need the expertise and services of a professional; Cooperative Publisher may be right for you. Cooperative Publishing uses the expertise of published authors, editors, marketers and a small press to assist the writer in each step of publishing, from an idea to a finished story, usually as much or as little as you need. Our authors have told us they liked Cooperative Publishing because they still had full control, but were being advised and guided by professionals. One of the features that our authors said helped them decide on Cooperative Publishing was that they could have their printed book within a short period of time, rather than waiting sometimes 18 months or more with a larger Publishing House. They were also happy to have someone sending out review copies, setting up book signings and web sites and doing other marketing, while they were choosing what they wanted to do. Most

Cooperative Publishers will only take works they feel are marketable as their name will be listed as the publisher. This also makes your work more credible to the rest of the publishing world and if you wish, you can still continue to try to sell your book to another publisher. Remember: Even with Cooperative Publishing, you always own the copyright and the book is yours to do with as you choose.

What Ever You Decide,

it has been wonderful taking this Writing Journey with you and

WE WISH YOU GOOD WRITING AND MUCH SUCESS!

Writing Map 12

TRIP REVIEW

Map Directions

Learn All You Can About the Writing Industry & Your Genré

Submit A Properly Prepared A Manuscript To The Right Editor

Use All the Resources Available — Libraries, Bookstores & The Internet

Treat Writing As A Business - Always Act As A Professional

Travel Instructions — Did You?

❑ Find your Genré

❑ Decide: Agent, Publisher, Self-Publishing, Cooperative Publishing or just for Family and Friends

❑ Make Lists for marketing your work from Writer's Market, Literary Marketplace and Publisher's Weekly

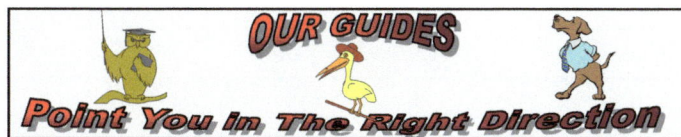

OUR GUIDES Point You in The Right Direction

It's Wise to Know Who is publishing what and why

Editors chirp when manuscripts are well presented

Publishing is a Business - Helpful Authors can make their Book the leader of the pack

Walk past a Bookstore and Picture Your Book in the Window under the Title

BEST SELLER

Tracking Log For _____
Book Name

Sent To:

PUBLISHER	ADDRESS	ZIP CODE
EDITOR'S NAME	PASSED ON TO	TEL: #	FAX #
EMAIL ADDRESS	DATE SENT	FOLLOW UP DATE

RESPONSE

ADDITIONAL INFORMATION

Sent To:

PUBLISHER	ADDRESS	ZIP CODE
EDITOR'S NAME	PASSED ON TO	TEL: #	FAX #
EMAIL ADDRESS	DATE SENT	FOLLOW UP DATE

RESPONSE

ADDITIONAL INFORMATION

Sent To:

PUBLISHER	ADDRESS	ZIP CODE
EDITOR'S NAME	PASSED ON TO	TEL: #	FAX #
EMAIL ADDRESS	DATE SENT	FOLLOW UP DATE

RESPONSE

ADDITIONAL INFORMATION

Sent To:

PUBLISHER	ADDRESS	ZIP CODE
EDITOR'S NAME	PASSED ON TO	TEL: #	FAX #
EMAIL ADDRESS	DATE SENT	FOLLOW UP DATE

RESPONSE

ADDITIONAL INFORMATION

FINAL WORD FROM OUR AUTHORS

We traveled this long road together and now that we have completed our journey;

We APPLAUD YOU!

You made a commitment and followed through; in spite of the bumpy roads,

difficult and unfamiliar terrain, detours and seemingly never ending miles.

Your finished story can now be the beginning of a new journey –

one that leads to new heights of accomplishment—

maybe even the best seller list.

As we leave you at your final destination we remind you that:

There's lots of good information at our web site:www.goldenquillpress.com

Many such successful journeys are possible

The techniques you've learned in this book will hopefully provide the tools

for many successful adventures

You are only limited by your own imagination

We look forward to traveling with you again!

And now a word from Our Guides:

Remember WHO you are - The Writer!

Sing Your OWN Praises - I Finished My Story

Bark for Success— YOU DESERVE IT!

ALERT— ALERT!

Our Wise Writing Guides AGREE
You are a BEST SELLER in OUR BOOK!

Thank you for traveling with…"From an Idea... to Your Finished Story"

Words Related to Writing

A

Advance – The amount paid to a writer by a publisher before a book is published. The advance is generally deducted from royalties earned from sales of the finished book.

Agent – A person who represents and acts on behalf of writers.

All rights – The rights contracted to a publisher (magazines, books) to permit the use of a writer's work any time, in any form without paying additional royalties.

Antagonists – A person (characters) who competes with or opposes another. An opponent or adversary.

Assignment – The contract between a writer and editor that confirms dates the writer will complete a project and fees to be paid the writer.

Autobiography – The story of one's own life written or dictated by oneself.

B

Book developer/packager – A business that plans and produces all elements of a book for publishers and producers.

Biography – An account of a person's life written by another.

By-line – The author's name on a published work.

C

Character – A person in a story or play.

Cliché – A trite expression or idea.

Climax – A decisive turning point or action.

Clips – Copies of a writer's work that has been published.

C

Confidant – The person to whom the main character would express undisclosed information the reader needs to know

Conflict – To clash or to be in opposition.

Contemporary – Relating to writing that reflects current trends, themes, and subjects.

Copy – Manuscript pages before being set in type.

Copy editing – The line by line editing of a manuscript.

Copyright – The lawful protection of a writer's work and considered to be in effect at the time of writing or by recording.

Cover letter – A one page, or brief letter to an editor sent with a manuscript.

D

Deadline – The date when a writer's work must be ready.

Denouement – The outcome, solution, or unraveling of a plot.

Description – Technique of describing or picturing by way of words.

Dialogue – The passages of talk or conversations in a play or story.

Disk copy – Circular plate on which data is stored; disk copy of a manuscript.

Draft – First or rough copies of a story, article, or other material.

E

Editing – To revise and make ready a manuscript

Editor – A person who's work is procuring and editing manuscripts

E-mail – Mail sent electronically by a computer.

Epiphany ending – The end of a story that gives the reader a sense of understanding and insight.

Exposition – The writing that explains facts, ideas, who characters are, the setting and related information.

F

Fair use – A provision in copyright law that allows the use of short quotes or passages to be used from copyrighted work.

Fiction – A story or other work of the imagination and portraying imaginary characters and events.

First serial rights – The right to publish materials for the first time before it is in book form.

Flashback – Filling in details in a story to let the reader know something that happened in the past. Also called back story

Flash forward – A device in writing that prepares the reader for events to come without going into specific details. Also called foreshadowing.

Free writing – Unrestrained writing that allows ideas to flow. Also called clustering or brainstorming. Methods of generating fresh ideas.

G

Galleys – The first set of proofs of a manuscript before being prepared in page form.

Genré – A category or type of fiction: Horror, western, romance, science fiction, etc....

H

Hard copy – A copy of a manuscript printed from a computer.

Hook – The lead into a story that keeps the reader interested. To hook or grab interest.

I

Imprint – A publisher's line. Example: Jan, an imprint of Robin House Publishers.

J

Juvenile fiction – stories for children ages 2 to 12.

Justify – Printing in line or flush. As when typing a manuscript, you may not want to justify right margins.

L

Lead-in – The beginning of a new scene.

Lead time – The time between planning a book and the publication date.

Literary agent – The person who represents an author, finds a publisher and negotiates contracts.

M

Mainstream – Fiction that has a prevailing and strong trend.

Manuscript – An author's unpublished work in typewritten pages. Abbreviated ms or mss (plural).

Mass market – Books that appeal to a wide readership and are sold in various outlets such as grocery, stationary and drug stores.

Masthead – A list of a magazine's staff members, their titles and departments.

Metaphor – A figure of speech where a word or phrase used for one thing is applied to another as in imagery. Example: A snowfall of white beard covered the old man's face.

Multiple submissions – Submitting more than one story to the same editor at the same time.

N

Narration – The events in a story related by the person telling the story.

Narrator – The person who tells a story.

O

One-time rights – Permission to reprint an author's work one time only.

Opposition – A person who resists, has an opposite stance or contradicts another.

Outline – A summary of a story or book contents.

P

Pace – The slowing down or speeding up of a story by punctuation, dialogue, or the author's style and use of language.

Pen name – Pseudonym an author chooses to use to conceal his or her own name.

Plot – The events scheme or plan of a story through which characters progress.

Premise – A short explanation of what the story is about.

Proofreading – The careful reading and correcting of errors in a manuscript using proofreader's marks.

Proposal – An offer to write a specific work.

Protagonist – The lead character in a story; the hero.

Public domain – Written material that is no longer copyrighted or has never been copyrighted.

Q

Query letter (a letter of inquiry) – A type of cover letter, usually one page, written to an editor in which the writer proposes a story, book, article, or an idea to the editor.

R

Rejection slip – A note from a publishing house that accompanies the return or refusal of an author's work.

Reprint rights – The right of a publisher to print an article or other work after it has been printed by another publication.

Resolution – The solution to a problem. A decision for future action. The end of a story made clear by an explanation.

Revision – To read carefully and correct, improve, update, or change a manuscript or other writing.

Royalties – A specified percentage paid for the work of an author.

S

SASE – Self addressed stamped envelope sent by an author for the return of work not accepted for publication.

Setting – The time period and location in which a story takes place.

Simultaneous submissions – Sending copies of a manuscript to more than one publisher at the time.

Simile – A figure of speech in which one thing is likened to another. Example: "A river of tears" or "Tears flowed like a river."

Slant – Writing a topic with a different approach.

Slush-pile – The stack of unsolicited manuscripts not likely to be accepted by a publisher.

Subplot – The secondary story running thread-like through the main plot.

Subsidiary rights – All the rights in addition to or other than book rights a published author may agree upon.

Synopsis – A brief summary of a story, usually a page or two, written to interest the editor in the complete work.

T

Tag – The words following the quoted dialogue of a character. Example: "Where are you?" he asked. "I am at the store," she said.

Theme – The central and dominant idea of a story or other work, also called the backbone, the message, or main thread.

Tone – The manner of writing that shows the attitude of the narrator.

Transition – A word, phrase, sentence, or paragraph that relates a preceding topic to a succeeding one. The connecting of one idea to the next.

U

Unsolicited submissions – Manuscripts sent to a publisher without an agency representation or that an editor did not ask to see.

V

Viewpoint – The position from which the narrator tells the story and how the story's action is meant to be seen by the reader.

AUTHORS BIOGRAPHIES

Francine Barish-Stern has been an author for over 40 years, and has received numerous awards for poetry and short stories. Her "Rainbow City" won first place and was published in "The Arts Newspaper." She has been a writer for newspapers and magazines and has worked on over 18 books including, "TELL IT TO THE FUTURE" and "NEW HORIZONS." She has recently finished her first full length novel "Code 47 to B R EV Force." Francine has developed writing programs for all ages and has created and designed materials for numerous businesses. She teaches writing, acting and co-wrote and produced, the play, "The WE Nobody Knows" for Crown Players. Also an accomplished business writer, she has specialized in seminars on telemarketing. Francine has recently added photography to her creative interests and has won major awards for her exhibits. Recently, her photograph, "Falls at the Bridge" was exhibited at the Art Museum of Western Virginia. All her art work are produced exclusively as Art on Gold and can be seen at Creations in Roanoke Virginia. .

Bobbi R. Madry, Educational Director for The Write Source and Golden Quill Press also serves as consultant, author and editor. During her career which has spanned more than 50 years, she has also served as senior editor of numerous books and educational publications for major New York City publishers. She has also written book reviews for national magazines. Bobbi served as Associate Publisher for a New York newspaper where she also mentored aspiring writers. She has received numerous awards for writing and community service. Bobbi teaches writing and poetry and holds degrees in the Arts and Behavioral Sciences. Her published works: Human Relations For Business - A Vocational Dictionary - The Job Seeker's Guide - Love Makes The Difference - Work Force 2000 (co-author) - The Professional Models Handbook (co-author). She has been the co-author and editor for Tell it to the Future and New Horizons as well editor of over 18 books published by Golden Quill Press, and is presently authoring several new books.

Books By Golden Quill Press

CODE 47 to BREV Force
By: F.Barish-Stern

The adventures of The BREV Force: College Students fighting to defeat the evils of Controller, a renegade computer virus, threatening to take over the world

TELL IT TO THE FUTURE
BY: Francine R. Cefola (F.Barish-Stern) & Bobbi R. Madry

TELL IT TO THE FUTURE-Have I Got A Story For You ... about the Twentieth Century leaves personal messages with timelines and stories about our hopes, dreams, or events that impacted on, or changed our lives. Each story focuses on events from a specific decade of the twentieth century with descriptions that reflect the color of the times. Some are witty, some filled with wisdom, while others pull at your heart strings.

LOVE MAKES A DIFFERENCE -
BY: Mary Bianchini and Bobbi Madry

Arriving as an immigrant with her mother in the early 1900's, Mary grew up to become one of the most influential figures in Rockland County, N.Y. Honored by four Presidents and in the Congressional Record, Mary shares her advice about family, community service and reaching her dreams.

NEW HORIZONS -
Life's Poetic Connections
BY: Francine R. Cefola (F. Barish-Stern)
& Bobbi R. Madry

Poetry is the art that speaks to our hearts and minds. Like a beautiful painting or a musical composition, this collection of poetry will take you into worlds limited only by your imagination... from the splendor of a sunset to tasting candy, to memories from a rocking chair ... **Let These Poems Take You To Your Own New Horizons!!**

CHALLENGING MESSAGES
FROM BEYOND

BY: Marjorie Struck

Does the Spiritual World have a message for us? Can we learn to understand that communication? Marjorie Struck certainly believes . This is her personal story of how a message form Beyond changed her life. Informative, at times shocking, but ultimately a journey that reveals a side of the spiritual world that can transform you-forever. Marjorie invites you along to witness how this revelation helped her understand the connection between life and beyond- and how souls in the after life help us to find the Light!

COMPASSION'S LURE

BY: Kathleen Lukens

This is the story of a visionary. Kathy Lukens founder of Camp Venture - advocate for all people with special needs stood up for the rights and deeds of those who could not fight for themselves. With words backed by tireless efforts, Kathy made the impossible happen for the developmentally disabled- a home and the proper attention to their needs. She was truly one of the Great Women of our times.

the GRANPA SPIDER stories

BY: Granpa Spider

A delightful story for children of all ages. Granpa Spider weaves a web of adventure and intrigue, mystery and fun! Along with his Arachnid friends, Penelope, The Colonel ,   and others we journey into the exciting world of the web. As Shamrock McGee says, "May the wind be at your web. May your web be in the trees. May cicada be chattering. May there be a host of bees, And, may the web that you spin be serving all your needs... "

MAE SINGS
ABOUT SHORT VOWELS

BY: Karen A. Coleman

"Mae Sings About Short Vowels," was developed by Karen Coleman, as a method for teaching music, while learning vowel sounds. The book uses songs and a vowel recognition technique in an interactive way to help students improve reading skills while learning musical notes

OPENING THE DOOR
TO A BRIGHTER FUTURE

BY: Daniel Windheim

After writing and publishing," It's Not All Black And White" which dealt with the experiences of my son, Dan ,sustaining a traumatic brain injury and the efforts he made to recover and build a productive life, we decided that many of the lessons both Dan and I learned from that experience might have relevance to others recovering from injuries or illnesses. We therefore set out to write a book detailing ten key strategies that could help individuals in their recovery efforts and to share the experiences of some survivors as they struggle to return to a healthy life. As Dan notes'" There is not time to waste focusing on the negative, but we need to take what we have and make the most out of things."

THE POEM BOOK

BY: Daniel Windheim

A brain injury victim of a car accident young Daniel Windheim's life is turned upside down. He turns to poetry to express his frustration, anger and and to take the reader on a beautiful journey through recuperation and new life challenges. Daniel Windheim is truly a shining hero, overcoming life's worst experience. "I remain practical; but a realist, and accept what I am. Life is good, and there is goodness in life."

SWEET MERCY

BY: Rebecca H. Cofer

Katherine Ryder peels away the decades of family secrets to tell her story of growing up in Fairburn, Georgia at the turn of the century - 1900. She battles many obstacles to free herself from small town life and her autocratic mother and moves to Atlanta. In the big city she is betrayed by the man she loves. But her generous heart and hard work pay off, bringing her joy and fulfillment in the end.

THERE IS HOPE

BY: Debby Paine

There Is Hope is a collection of religious poetry about the struggles, pains questions and fears we all face. Debby's love of family, church and community is portrayed as she searches for and reaches toward God to find hope. These poems from the heart-for the heart, will reach out to everyone searching for hope. " Reach for it. Hold on to it. 'Hope is There.' "

Other books marketed by Golden Quill Press:

YOU ARE WHAT YOU WEAR

BY:William Thourlby

"First impressions" are lasting. YOU ARE WHAT YOU WEAR will help you make the right "first impression." Develop skills that are cost effective because they not only increase the quality of life in the workplace, contribute to employee morale and embellish the company image, they play a major role in developing a person's self image and generating profits. The lack of these skills can be highly visible and costly for any person or company in every day and age.

PASSPORT TO POWER

BY: William Thourlby

Part practical, part primer, part visionary, Passport to Power, gives the reader background and formulas to follow to acquire and master international communication skills and provide the keys to unlocking human potential for success as a leader in the new global village of today.

TELL IT TO THE FUTURE

Have I got A Story For You…
About the Twentieth Century

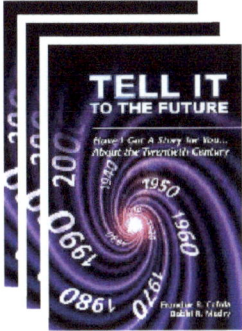

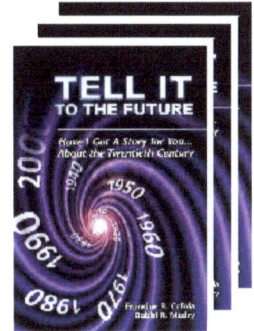

Stories to make

You laugh, Stories to make

You cry

Stories to bring

Back memories of a Time Gone By

Stories of a time that

Most of us never knew

Coming to America…

Going off to war

Just to name a few

These stories vividly paint a portrait of America during the decades

Of the 20th Century…

Am America you'll never forget

GREAT REFERENCE and RESOURCE Book
For the Twentieth Century

BE SURE YOU

TELL IT TO THE FUTURE

Order at www.goldenquillpress.com

www.ingramcontent.com/pod-product-compliance
Lightning Source LLC
Chambersburg PA
CBHW042015080426
42735CB00002B/64